前世

The Past

图书在版编目（ＣＩＰ）数据

东堂子胡同75号院：蔡元培故居的前世今生 ／ 蔡元培
故居纪念馆，富华国际集团编著． — 北京：文物出版社，
2011.10

ISBN 978-7-5010-3287-7

Ⅰ．①东… Ⅱ．①蔡… ②富… Ⅲ．①蔡元培
（1867～1940）－故居－介绍 Ⅳ．①K878.23

中国版本图书馆CIP数据核字（2011）第197504号

东堂子胡同75号院｜蔡元培故居的前世今生
No.75 Yard DongTangZiHuTong AlleyWay
The Past and Present of Cai Yuanpei's Former Residence

装帧设计　　刘　远

责任印制　　梁秋卉

责任编辑　　张小舟

出版发行　文物出版社

地　　址　北京市东直门内北小街2号楼

邮　　编　100007

网　　址　http://www.wenwu.com

　　　　　E-mail:web@wenwu.com

制版印刷　北京圣彩虹制版印刷技术有限公司

开　　本　889毫米×1194毫米　1/12

印　　张　15.5

版　　次　2011年10月第1版

印　　次　2011年10月第1次印刷

书　　号　ISBN 978-7-5010-3287-7

定　　价　168.00元

蔡元培（1868-1940年），字鹤卿，号子民，浙江绍兴人。
1917年出任北京大学校长
Cai Yuanpei (1868-1940), whose courtesy name was Heqing
and sobriquet was Jiemin (Lone Citizen), was born in Shaoxing,
Zhejiang Province. He took up the post of the Chancellor of
Peking University in 1917

主　编	赵　勇	
顾　问	周其凤	罗哲文
	陈丽华	
策　划	渠晓玲	
编委会	王守元	王铁生
	周　东	渠晓玲
执　笔	蔡大成	
摄　影 （今生部分）	宏　铭	张　纬

感谢北京大学、新文化运动纪念馆对本书出版的大力支持，特此鸣谢！

目录

Contents

The Past

东堂子胡同
75

篇首语
Foreword

赵勇 | 富华国际集团总裁
Chiu Yung
President of Fu Wah International Group

◆　我的办公室离蔡元培先生的故居不远，步行到这里用不了10分钟的时间，顺着东堂子胡同西口向里走，没几步便会看到这座灰墙青瓦的小院，在喧嚣中独守一片清静。暗红色小门，门楣上贴着"东堂子胡同75"的门牌，黑漆的门框的西边，长条的灰砖里砌着一块汉白玉的方石，上面清晰地刻着"蔡元培故居"的字样。

◆　推开院门，此刻的光线斜洒下来，在静谧的胡同和简朴的房子上投下了斑驳的树影。这处院落便是蔡元培先生1917年担任北京大学校长时的住所。坐北朝南的三进四合院，似乎还寻得着主人的身影。沿着廊子进去，在院落的最深处，一座汉白玉雕的先生的塑像正以他深邃的目光，注视着这个辛亥百年后现代的中国。

◆　东堂子胡同75号院，记录了蔡元培先生的一段生活轨迹，截留了蔡先生与五四运动那一特殊历史时期的岁月点滴。这所看似再普通不过的四合院因了92年前点燃无数沸腾的心灵，摇动五四摇篮而青史留名。

◆　此刻我就站在先生的塑像前，或许我无法穿越回到那个风云际会的年代，无缘在血火年代与先生谋面并受教终生，但60年后我却注定在北大求学浸染其精神魂魄。更加庆幸得的是，在一个世纪之后我竟有机会可以为蔡先生的历史剪影保留这一方净土，这是作为北大一员的我的荣幸与责任。

◆ 由于历史的原因，蔡元培故居几十年来一直被当成普通民居使用，及至20世纪90年代末期，东堂子胡同75号院里已经住进了14户人家，使得原本就拥挤的小院更加不堪重负。全然看不到一丝故居当年的格局和影子，接待社会各界参观更是无从提起。

◆ 2000年北京市政府启动了金宝街旧城危房拆迁改造项目，使得对蔡元培故居的保护和修缮工作提到了政府的议事日程中来。故居不仅是金宝街的一个文物保护单位，也是整个金宝街的一个亮点。从2007年开始，在北京市及东城区两级文物部门的指导下，蔡元培故居修复工程正式启动。可以说，蔡元培故居的保护和修复是一个历史性的过程，在这个过程中，富华国际集团经历了对遗址保护的规划、独立存在以及之后修复和陈列等多个阶段，付出了极大的心智和努力。从拆迁到规划，从修缮到纪念馆展品的收集，耗资数千万元。经过两年多的努力，2009年5月，终于将一个充满故事和历史感的蔡元培故居纪念馆回馈给了社会。

◆ 时至今日，东堂子胡同75号院蔡元培故居被列为北京市第八批市级文物保护单位，成为免费参观的爱国主义教育基地。看到故居中人来人往我很高兴，我以为让历史活下去，是对历史最好的回报。今年的10月10日是辛亥革命百年纪念日，蔡元培先生是辛亥的元老，在这样特殊的日子里，我想我应该把这段历史记录下来，于是便有了这本《东堂子胡同75号院 —— 蔡元培故居的前世今生》最初的构想。

东堂子胡同75号院 | 蔡元培故居的前世今生
No. 75 Yard in Dongtangzihutong Alleyway
The Past and Present of Cai Yuanpei's Former Residence

009

◆ 记得梁思成、林徽因在《平郊建筑杂录》中写过，建筑本身具有一种"建筑意"，而这正是建筑的灵魂所在。"无论哪一个巍峨的古城楼，或一角倾颓的殿基的灵魂里，无形中都在诉说，乃至于歌唱，时间上漫不可信的变迁。由温雅的儿女佳话，到流血成渠的杀戮。它们所说的'意'的确是'诗'与'画'的。"

◆ 蔡元培故居又何尝不是，它的每个角落里都仿佛散发着那个时代的气息。依原貌恢复的卧室里陈设简单，摆放的单人床上铺着蓝底白花的床单，衣架上挂着一件青色的长袍，好像主人刚刚外出的样子。正午的阳光透过书房的窗户，直射在窗前书桌上那台老式的英文打字机上。书桌上文房四宝，还留有当年蔡元培先生编写的《教育心理学大意》的手稿，依稀还散发着淡淡的墨香。书房的一角，一个老旧的转轮拨号电话机也是1918年产的老古董，拿起听筒，里面竟然能听到清晰的拨号的声音。一切都恍如隔世，仿佛它的主人从未走远……

◆ 我似乎也有些痴迷这样的感觉，所以很多个午后，我常常会不由自主地从故居旁边的大厦里步行到此，看三两个游人静静地在院中，或细语，或感慨，或沉思。每每这个时候，我总是会为自己之前所有的付出感到骄傲和自豪，我无意中走进蔡元培先生身后的历史并使之延续，让那段历史在这座宅子里凝聚，继续感染和启迪后世，不能不说这是一种冥冥之中的注定和安排。

◆ 东堂子胡同75号院，就像一部记录蔡元培先生在特定时代下展现在历史舞台上的史书，流传久远……

My office is only ten minutes' walk away from Mr. Cai Yuanpei's former residence. Walk straight into the Dongtangzihutong alleyway from its western exit until you see a small yard with grey walls and mossy tiles standing in tranquility and surrounded by bustling cities. There is a small scarlet door with a door plate written "No. 75 Dongtangzihutong Alleyway" on the lintel, and with black-painted frame. In the west of the door placed a long brick, in which a square white marble with the clear carving of "The former residence of Cai Yuanpei" was built.

As the door of the courtyard is opened, light sprays over the silent alleyway and the house and trees cast their mottled shadows. It was the house that Mr. Cai Yuanpei lived in when he served as the president of Peking University in 1917. It seems that the three-row quadrangle courtyard which faces south still reserves the memories of the owner. Walk deeper along the corridor, you may find a white marble sculpture of Mr. Cai who insightfully gazes at the modern China after the Revolution of 1911.

The yard at No.75 Dongtangzihutong alleyway is a record of Cai's life and the special days during the May 4th Movement. This simple and ordinary quadrangle courtyard is remembered for it awoke millions of Chinese and stimulating the Movement 92 years ago.

Now I am standing in front of Mr. Cai's sculpture, and I cannot go back to the revolutionary days to benefit from him in person, but it is destined that I would learn from him when I studied in Peking University 60 years later. What's more, I am honored with the opportunity to reserve the house bearing the memories of Mr. Cai, which is indeed an honor and responsibility for any member of the university.

Throughout the history, Mr. Cai's former residence has been used as common dwellings for several decades. By the end of the 1990s, altogether 14 families have moved in the yard which turned more crowded. The original style and layout of the yard disappeared, not to mention the preparation for receiving visitors.

In 2000, the municipal government of Beijing carried out a reconstruction and demolition project of dangerous houses in Jinbao Street, putting the protection and repair of Cai's former residence on the governmental agenda. Cai's former residence is not only a protected historic site, but a distinguishing feature in Jinbao Street. In 2007, the renovation project of Cai's former residence was initiated under the direction of cultural relic departments of both Beijing municipal government and Dongcheng District. We can say that the project is a process of historic importance, during which Fu Wah International Group has devoted much efforts to the plan, independence and the later repair and display of the relics. It cost tens of millions from the phase of demolition to planning, from repairing to the collection of the displaying items. By May 2009, a brand new Cai Yuanpei's former residence full of stories and histories was finally presented to the society.

Now the former residence situated at No. 75 Dongtangzihutong alleyway is among the eighth group of municipal units of protected cultural relics, a patriotic education site free to the public. I am glad to see here crowded because the best gift to history, I think, is to make it continue. October 10th this year marks the centennial of the Revolution of 1911 and Mr. Cai was one of the leaders, I suppose to record the history on such a special day, which brings about the initial construct of this book, No. 75 Dongtangzihutong Alleyway---the Past and the Present of Cai Yuanpei's Former Residence.

In the Records of Buildings in Suburban Beijing written by Liang Sicheng and Lin Huiyin, buildings have in their own a kind of building spirit which is the very soul of the building. "All lofty ancient gate towers or decadent hall bases are telling in whisper even singing the changes in time; from soft love stories to cruel slaughters. All these are poetic and vivid."

Cai Yuanpei's former residence is the same. Each of its corners seems to haunt the breath of that age. The items recovered as the original such as the blue sheet with white flowers spreading on the single bed, as well as the cyan long gown hung on the hanger seemingly indicating that the owner left just now. An old English typewriter on the desk before the window is exposed to the sunshine at noon. On the table, you can find the manuscripts of Mr. Cai's The Gist of Pedagogic Psychology which still smells the fragrance of Chinese ink. Turn to the corner, there is an antique dialing telephone made in 1918; once picking it up, you can hear the clear sound of dialing. All these items made visitors feel like being close to their owners.

Fascinated with this feeling, I often, in afternoons, subconsciously wander here from the building beside, seeing several visitors standing in the yard, whispering, sighing or pondering by themselves. Every such moment I can hardly control the overflow of the proud of what I have done before. In coincidence, I am involved in Mr. Cai's history and make it continue and accumulate in the yard, educating and enlightening the later generations. I have to say it is really destined arrangements.

The NO. 75 Dongtangzihutong Alleyway is a history book about Mr. Cai's life in special times, which will be handed down forever.

东堂子胡同75号院 | 蔡元培故居的前世今生
No. 75 Yard in Dongtangzihutong Alleyway
The Past and Present of Cai Yuanpei's Former Residence

013

序
Preface

罗哲文 | 著名古建筑学家
Luo Zhewen
Distinguished Architect
of Ancient Chinese Architecture

◆ 历代的中国建筑和城市规划，无论是在技术、艺术还是其他诸多方面，形成了中国特有的文化气质和建筑特点。但在封建社会，工艺匠人社会地位低，且限于文化程度，历代的建筑经验难以形成可世代相传的文字，从而束缚了中国建筑的发展。自20世纪初，教育家蔡元培先生开始大力倡导近代建筑艺术，先生的"思想自由，兼容并包"的新教育理念影响并启迪着先师梁思成先生，为他投身中国建筑研究奠定了思想基础和坚定的信心。

◆ 中国是世界文明古国，北京又是举世闻名的历史文化名城，这些历史文物、古建筑和名人故居，正是古国的文明象征，历史文化名城的标志。试想，如果一个城市、一个国家，没有了自己的古代文化和历史底蕴作为支撑这个城市、这个国家的精神，那居住其中的人们，是否也会因为或缺了这种支柱而失去一份精神上的依靠？自1940年师从梁思成先生，我便一直向他学习并协助先生进行中国文物古迹、古建筑的保护、调查和研究工作，同时也是为了能够以己绵薄之力传承中华文化。1949年年初，随着北平的和平解放，我有幸能继续跟随先生，从事北平城内古老建筑的保护和研究。历经了多年的建筑研究工作后，使我对北京古建筑和名人故居的一殿一阁、一廊一亭、一山一石、一砖一瓦、一花一木都产生了深厚的感情，总是怕它们受到不应有的损害，进而总要想方设法去保护它们。

◆　鹤卿先生的故居我是了解的，那是一个典型的老北京三进式四合院。但在早先去的时候，小小的院子里面，竟满满当当的住着十多户的人家，而各家又划地盖房，小小院落里已无多少下脚的地方。 先生当年将此处作为一个新文化运动的酝酿地，新学术的小沙龙，而所有这些点滴的记忆，也早已随着各家的袅袅炊烟，随着时光的流逝点点散去……

◆　鹤卿先生在我印象中，是近代中国新文化和新教育倡导最杰出的领导之一，虽说他出身科举（清翰林出身），但对新学术的执着，对新人的栽培，却和先师思成先生有很多的共通之处。思成先生生前也是对鹤卿先生异常尊敬，常感慨他是为"现代教育第一人"，自谦中国建筑史的思想基础，多半来源于鹤卿先生的倡导。因此，作为后人，当我第一次看到富华国际集团工程部认真而诚恳的送来鹤卿先生故居修复图纸方案时，心中除了欣喜之外，更多的是一份感动！

◆　时至今日，北京仍有不少重要史迹、名人故居、历史文物、古建筑需要去调查发现。我们保护文物和故居的目的，是要发挥其作用，并不是单纯的为保护而保护。关于发挥作用的问题，我以为保护的"度"很关键，譬如有价值的古建筑或是名人故居，绝不能当一般房屋去利用，更不能当工厂车间去利用，而是要发挥它的历史、艺术、科学研究方面的价值。除了直接开放参观之外，

东堂子胡同75号院 | 蔡元培故居的前世今生
No.75 Yard in Dongtangzuhutong Alleyway
The Past and Present of Cai Yuanpei's Former Residence

015

还要提供间接的资料，如历史图片、典籍资料、参观游览介绍等。

◆ 我曾以为，当前很多注重城市现代建设的设计规划者，对中国传统城市建筑重视不够，但是富华国际集团报来的故居修复图纸细致而严谨，可以看出集团对修复工程的重视。修复的图纸中，大到整体方案的规划、现居住居民的搬迁安置，小到展出文物和原建筑瓦当的建档保存，无一不体现出对鹤卿先生的尊敬和对故居的爱护！是真正意义上的爱国之举！

◆ 鹤卿先生的东堂子胡同故居历经近一个世纪的风雨，如今已经修葺完整，不仅把之前因为居民私自改建而受到破坏的房屋按照历史原状进行了恢复和修缮；同时还利用传统建筑的工艺方法进行加固，尽可能保存文物实物，从而使故居得到了更好的保护，做到了真正意义上"不改变原状"。仅这点，无论是在过去还是现在，都是难能可贵的一个善举！而今，作为一位从事古建筑研究70余载、热爱中国传统文化的老卒，能为这本《东堂子胡同75号院 —— 蔡元培故居的前世今生》作序，未尝不感到是作为后人纪念先生的一种荣幸。这本书，将不光向后人讲述了鹤卿先生令人尊崇的一生，更将会把中国的传统建筑文化，和先生"育国家之良民"的思想，代代相传！是以为序，以之请教观众方家高明，并借以为对这一重要名人故居修缮完整公开开放之祝贺。

罗哲文

Throughout history, ancient Chinese architecture and urban planning have formed China's unique cultural and architectural features, no matter in technology, art or other aspects. However, due to the low social status and poor education of the artisans in feudal society, experience from ancient architecture has not been put into words, which otherwise can be passed on from generation to generation. This impedes the development of Chinese architecture. Since the early 20th Century, Cai Yuanpei, a great educator, began to advocate modern architecture, and his new educational philosophy of " Freedom of Thoughts, an All-bracing Openness to Ideas " also influenced and inspired Mr. Liang Sicheng, which laid the ideological foundation and gave firm faith for the latter to engage in the study of Chinese architecture.

These historical relics, ancient buildings and former residences of celebrities are a symbol of ancient civilization and a logo of historical and cultural city, as China is one of the ancient civilizations in the world and Beijing is a famous historical and cultural city worldwide. Just think about this: if a city or a country loses its own ancient culture and historical heritage, which are its spiritual pillars, will the people there lose a kind of spiritual reliance just because of missing this pillar? Since 1940, under the guidance of Mr. Liang Sicheng, I have assisted him in the conservation and researches of China's relics and ancient buildings and contributed my pygmy efforts to the inheritance of Chinese culture. At the beginning of 1949, as Peking was liberated, I had the opportunity to follow Mr. Liang to conserve and study the ancient architecture inside Peking city.

The former residence of Mr. Cai, to my mind, is a typical three-row quadrangle courtyard. But in the past, the small yard was full of more than 10 households to its capacity and, as each household built his own houses, there was no room left to get a foothold. At that time, my teacher took this place as a cradle for the New Culture Movement and a small salon for the new academy. All these pieces of memories have long been dispersed as different people moved in and out of the yard and as time went by.

In my mind, Mr. Cai is the first modern Chinese who advocates new culture and new education. In terms of academic dedication and student cultivation, he shares a lot with my teacher, Mr. Liang Sicheng, although he was born and bred under the system of imperial examination (Imperial Academy in the Qing Dynasty). During his lifetime, my teacher also paid great respect to Mr. Cai and often said humbly that most of his thoughts about Chinese architectural history stemmed from "the first modern educator", Mr. Cai. Therefore, as a later generation, I was moved as well as overjoyed when I first saw the drawing for the restoration of Mr. Cai's former residence submitted seriously and sincerely by the Engineering Department of Fu Wah International Group.

Up to the present, Beijing still boasts many important historical sites, former residence of celebrities, historical relics and ancient buildings for further discovery and survey. We protect these cultural relics and the former residences with the aim to exerting their roles, not simply for the sake of protection and conservation. As far as their roles are concerned, I hold that the "degree" of protection is rather critical; for instance, valuable old buildings or former residences are expected not to be used as a common house or a workshop but to play their historical, artistic, and scientific research parts. In addition to directly open these former residences to the public, other indirect information are also expected to be provided, such as historical photographs, books, records and sightseeing introductions, etc.

I formerly thought that, many urban designers and planners who take construction of modern city seriously may fail to have a good mastery of traditional Chinese architectural culture or pay enough attention to traditional Chinese urban architecture; but these delicate and rigorous drawings for former residence renovation provided by Fu Wah International Group show the Group's great attention to the renovation. These drawings, from the overall planning, the relocation of the residents, to the file preservation of displayed artifacts and original buildings, fully reflect the Group's respect to Mr. Cai and their care for the former residence. Their earnest attitude indicates that they are really patriotic!

Mr. Cai's former residence at Dongtangzihutong alleyway, going through a century of rain and storm, has now been renovated. The houses damaged by unauthorized construction has been restored and repaired in accordance with their former appearance and reinforced by employing traditional building techniques and methods. The cultural relics have been preserved as much as possible, so as to make better protection "without significant changes to the original state". Only this, both in the past and at present, is a rather commendable kind deed! Now, as an architect who has studied ancient buildings for more than 70 years and an old man who loves traditional Chinese culture, I feel honored to write this preface for the book- No. 75 Yard in Dongtangzihutong Alleyway - the Past and Present of Cai Yuanpei's Former Residence, as a commemoration of Mr. Cai. This book not only tells the following generations about his respectable life but also passes on the traditional Chinese architectural culture and Mr. Cai's concept of "educating good citizens for the country" from generation to generation! I wrote a preface for the book for consultation and suggestion of book readers and profession experts. Furthermore, and I want to express my congratulations to the completion of Cai Yuanpei's former residence restoration and it's opening to the public through this article.

校长风骨 薪火传承
President Cai Yuanpei's Spirit Passes on

周其凤 丨 北京大学校长
Zhou Qifeng the President of Peking University

◆ 20世纪初叶，中国大地风云际会，涌动着各类变革的思潮。一大批拨动中国历史琴弦的杰出人物，应运而生，在中国历史的演进中，扮演了极其重要的角色。北京大学被推上历史的舞台，在中国近现代史上，开风气之先，手握民主革命之利器，开创了中国历史崭新的篇章。

◆ 北京大学最引以为自豪的是为中国革命贡献了一系列标榜史册的名人。他们是中国共产党创始人和早期领导人陈独秀、李大钊。新文化运动的代表人物胡适，以及茅盾、马寅初、钱玄同、刘半农……他们创办的《新青年》杂志吹响了五四运动的号角，使北京大学成为近现代中国思想的良田沃土。

◆ 当然，在这里我们必须要记住一个重要的历史人物 — 蔡元培。蔡元培是北京大学的老校长，是北大民主进步的精神领袖。他是20世纪初中国资本主义教育制度的始创者。他明确提出废止忠君、尊孔、尚公、尚武、尚实的封建教育宗旨，开创了中国现代教育理念与教育制度的先河。同时也为五四运动的爆发，创造了制度条件。他的"思想自由、兼容并包"的主张，使北大成为新文化运动的发祥地、大本营，成为新民主主义革命的摇篮。

◆　蔡元培校长一生清廉。在北京大学任职期间，没有像其他教授那样在京城购置房产。而在四城之内的院落，均留下了蔡元培租住的故迹。早在1986年，北京市东城区政府就将东堂子胡同75号，挂牌确认为蔡元培故居，列为文物保护单位。但无奈的是，这个杂乱无章的院子，无法接待众多的参观寻访者，院内的居民也是不胜其累。一个窄小的门道内，居住着十四户居民，建筑物年久失修，很难让人想象这里曾是近代民主革命家、教育家、科学家蔡元培先生的故居。

◆　我在这里要特别感谢富华国际集团，他们在金宝街开发建设中，着力保护蔡元培故居，不但将故居内原有的十四户居民妥善安置，实现了文物的腾退；而且将故居精心修葺，整旧如旧，还原了历史。为北京大学、为全国人民保留下了一份珍贵的遗产，实在是功在当代，利在千秋。

◆　今次，富华国际集团又组织撰写了这本《东堂子胡同75号院 — 蔡元培故居的前世今生》，图文并茂地记录了蔡元培校长在故居的日子和所处的时代。文以人传，人以文传。相信这本书一定会对从事蔡元培研究、热爱景仰蔡元培先生伟大人格的人们提供有益的资粮。

周其凤

At the beginning of the 20th century, with the arrival of revolutionary days, various thoughts which proclaimed the principle of change emerged in China. An army of prominent people, who influenced China's history and played significant roles in the evolution of it, appeared at the right moment as the times required. As a pioneer of the revolution practice, Peking University entered the arena of modern and contemporary history, and its support of democratic revolution helped to open a new chapter of China's history.

What Peking University has extremely taken pride in is that it has contributed a lot of historically famous persons who worked for China's revolution, including Chen Duxiu and Li Dazhao, who were the founders of the Communist Party and leaders of it at the early stage; Hu Shi, a representative of the New Culture Movement; and Mao Dun, Ma Yinchu,

Qian Xuantong, and Liu Bannong, etc. They published a magazine- the New Youth, which sounded the bugle of the May Fourth Movement, and enabled Peking University to become the place of cultivating modern and contemporary thoughts in China.

With no doubt, here we should remember Cai Yuanpei, a significant historical personage. Cai Yuanpei was a former president of Peking University and a spiritual leader of the university in the progress towards democracy. He was the founder of capitalistic educational system of China in the early 20th century. He made a clear statement to raise an objection to feudal educational missions, which were being loyal to the emperor, respecting Confucius, highly valuing the collectivism, militarism and utilitarianism; meanwhile, he initiated the modern thoughts and system of education in China, which offered institutional conditions for the outbreak of the May Fourth Movement. His proposal of "free mind is open to all" allowed Peking University to become the birthplace and headquarters of the New Culture Movement, and the cradle of new democratic revolution.

President Cai Yuanpei remained honest and incorruptible all his life. During his tenure in Peking University, he did not purchase any estate in the capital like other professors did. Instead, he rent houses in different places around the city. As early as 1986, the NO.75 yard in Dongtangzihutong alleyway was recognized as Cai Yuanpei's former residence and defined as a protected cultural relic by the local government of Dongcheng District of Beijing. However, this yard was disordered and could not admit numerous visitors; at the same time, the residents who lived in the yard had been tired of the visiting. In this narrow alleyway there were over 14 households, and the building had been out of repair for ages. It is hard to imagine that, Mr. Cai Yuanpei, a capitalistic revolutionary, educator and scientist in modern China, once lived here.

Here I want to express my appreciation especially to Fu Wah International Group, because, in the construction of Jinbao Street, they not only exerted themselves to protect the former residence of Cai Yuanpei, but also properly resettled the 14 original households. They not only cleaned out the culture relic, but also repaired and renovated it carefully and restored its original appearance and history. Having helped to retain a precious heritage for Peking University and national people, they contribute a monumental merit that benefits the future.

This time again, Fu Wah International Group compiles the book, No. 75 Yard in Dongtangzihutong Alleyway- the Past and Present of Cai Yuanpei's Former Residence, which records the days of president Cai Yuanpei in the former residence and the times in which he lived, with lyrical words and photographs. Books are passed down by people and people become immortal in books. It is believed that this book will certainly offer beneficial knowledge to the one who conducts research on Cai Yuanpei or the one who loves and respects his great personality.

唯有精神永驻
Long Live Cai Yuanpei's Spirit

陈丽华 ｜ 全国政协港澳台侨委员会副主任
富华国际集团主席

Chan Laiwa, deputy head of Committee for
Liaison with Hong Kong, Macao, Taiwan and
Overseas Chinese of CPPCC, and president
of Fu Wah International Group

◆　蔡元培先生的一生华彩无数，他是民主革命家，是社会活动家，但更以职业教育家闻名于世。他一生历经风雨，却始终信守爱国和民主的政治理念，致力于废除封建主义的教育制度，奠定了我国新式教育制度的基础，为我国教育、文化、科学事业的发展作出了富有开创性的贡献。

◆　蔡元培先生被人们称为"学界泰斗"，官职也不低，但他非常俭朴，在北京任职多年，竟没置房，一直是租房住。他先后在西城、宣武、东城住过，唯独把东堂子胡同75号院确定为他的故居，概因五四运动在这里策源。

◆　5月4日下午，数千学生在天安门前举行示威大会，人群不断扩大，组成浩浩荡荡的游行大军。此时的蔡元培坐镇家中，火烧火燎的政府官员把电话打到家中，要求他召回学生。"学生爱国运动，我不忍制止。"他这样回答。当晚，蔡元培回北京大学商讨营救事宜时说："被捕同学的安全，是我的事，一切由我负责。"

◆　可以想见，若时光倒退90多年，这里应有不亚于烽火连天的危急斗争，也有一个为人师者的铮骨与仁怀。"以一个校长身份，而能领导那所大学对一个民族、一个时代，起到转折作用的，除蔡元培而外，恐怕找不出第二个。"这是美国哲学家、教育家杜威对蔡元培先生的赞叹。

◆　如果说北大红楼是蔡元培在历史前台活动的中心，则东堂子胡同75号就是他的精神后院。

◆　我也有幸走近蔡先生的精神后院。1986年，这里被列为东城区文物保护单位。但由于历史原因，故居几十年来一直被居民使用，建筑年久失修，无从接待社会各界参观。2000年底，在金宝街市政开发建设中，富华国际集团作为开发建设单位搬迁了院内14户居民，拆除了违章建筑，实现

了文物腾退，为保护利用创造了条件。2007年7月，修缮工程开始。2009年5月10日，时隔蔡元培先生离京86年之后，东堂子胡同75号院第一次真正以蔡元培故居的名义向世人敞开了大门。

◆　城市的明天需要发展，但城市的昨天也需要保护，因为一座城市一旦割裂了它与历史文化的联系，无论它怎样的奢华和现代，都逃脱不了它的空洞。

◆　名人故居就是这样一个由现实通向历史的窗口。人们常说建筑是凝固的音乐，从某种意义上也道出了名人故居的人文价值。作为一种人文环境，具有中国传统民居建筑风格的名人故居往往具有一种特殊的意味，它往往是一种文化的孕育场，历史的复原地，对人的成长和生活断面的截留，具有某种特殊而潜在的影响功能。

◆　蔡元培故居的修复不同于一般的四合院建造，要做到按照历史原状恢复和修缮，就一定要尽可能多地使用原有的砖瓦及梁架结构。在修复之前，我们特意请老专家们对施工人员进行了故居保护培训。被拆下来的老砖瓦，我们都精心收集，用纸一片片包好，

分门别类统一编号，重建时再一一对应修葺。

◆ 对于教育，我是外行，对于蔡元培先生的感慨，自然更不敢置喙。我唯愿尽心尽力去还原历史的一砖一瓦，让过去的一幕能荡起今人今事的心头一瞬。历史犹如我所钟情的紫檀一样，历久弥新，唯有时间能证明他们的价值。

◆ 唯愿蔡先生风骨永在。

Mr. Cai Yuanpei has a glorious life. He is a democratic revolutionist, a social activist, but is known more as a professional educator. Mr. Cai went through a lot of hardships and dangers, but he still held firmly the political faith in patriotism and democracy. He endeavored to abolish the feudalistic educational systems and lay a foundation for new ones in China, making groundbreaking contribution to the development of Chinese education, culture and science.

Mr. Cai was named "a leading authority in Chinese academic circles" holding a relatively high position, but he led a thrifty and simple life in Beijing. He rented instead of buying a house during his working life. Though once moved to Xicheng, Xuanwu and Dongcheng districts, he only took NO.75 yard in Dongtangzihutong alleyway as his home, probably because it was the birthplace of the May 4th Movement.

On that May 4th, thousands of students started a demonstration in front of Tian'anmen Square. The demonstration then turned to be a large parade as more and more people joined. Cai stayed at home then when panic officials called him to recall the students. However, Cai refused, "it is such a patriotic activity that I cannot bear to stop it." At night, he assured people when he went back to Peking University to discuss the rescue of those arrested students, "it is my duty to guarantee the safety of those arrested students, and I will take the responsibility."

We can imagine that, if we can go back to more than 90 years ago, this place is witnessing a fight no less dangerous than a war and the integrity and kindness of a teacher. John Dewey, an American philosopher and educator, highly praises Mr. Cai like this, "we can hardly find a second person in China except Cai Yuanpei who, as a university president, can make a transition for a nation and an era by leading the university."

If the Red House was the center of Cai's revolutionary activities, then NO.75 yard in Dongtangzihutong alleyway was his support in spirit.

I also had the honor to visit this "spiritual support". In 1986, it was defined as a protected cultural relic in Dongcheng district. However, throughout history, the house has been used by common residents for several decades and the building was out of repair for ages, so it can hardly be opened to the public. Until the end of 2000, FUHUA Group, as the developers in the municipal construction program in Jinbaojie Street, moved 14 households and demolished all unlawful buildings, recovering the cultural relics and creating conditions for the protection and utilization program. In July 2007, the repairing project was started, and on May 10th, 2009, which was 86 years since Cai left Beijing, NO. 75 yard in Dongtangzihutong alleyway, as Cai Yuanpei's Former Residence, was opened the first time to the public.

The future of cities needs development and the past also requires protection. Once the connection between its history and culture is broken, a city will inevitably become shallow no matter how prosperous and modern they look.

The former residences of famous figures are the very links between the

东堂子胡同75号院 | 蔡元培故居的前世今生
No. 75 Yard in Dongtangzihutong Alleyway
The Past and Present of Cai Yuanpei's Former Residence

027

present and the past. It is generally accepted that a building is a piece of static music which tells to some extent the cultural value of the residences of famous figures. These residences distinctive for their traditional Chinese building style have special significance, which are the birthplaces of specific culture and reflections of history. Moreover, they are the fragments of people's life, with some special and potential influence.

The repairing project of Cai Yuanpei's former residence, different from the construction of common quadrangle courtyards, requires to recover or renovate everything as the original,

and to use the original bricks and beam frame structures as well. Before renovation, we specially invited senior experts to give the constructors training about former residence protection. We wrapped deliberately each removed old tiles in paper and coded after categorizing them, and then move them back to the same position when repairing the house.

I know little in education and cannot make casual comments on Mr. Cai's achievements. However, I am obliged to devote myself to repairing each and every brick and tile of the house, so as to reproduce memories of the past in people now. Like the rosewood I love, history keeps itself fresh through all these years and only time can serve as the proof of their value.

May Cai's upright spirit last forever.

文化领袖 泰然襟怀

Part 1
A Broadmined Cultural Leader with Equanimity

蔡元培（1868－1940年），字鹤卿，号子民，浙江绍兴人。早年投身资产阶级民主革命，创立光复会，加入同盟会，曾担任中华民国临时政府第一任教育总长。1917年1月就任国立北京大学校长，实行"兼容并包，思想自由"的办学方针，对北大进行改革，把陈腐的旧北大改造成思想活跃、蓬勃向上的现代大学，使之成为新文化运动中心和五四运动的发祥地。后任国民政府常务委员、大学院院长、中央研究院院长等职，发起组织中国民权保障同盟，1940年3月5日在香港病逝。

Cai Yuanpei (1868-1940), whose courtesy name (zi) is Heqing and literary name (hao) Jiemin, was a native of Shaoxing, Zhejiang Province. When he was young, he threw himself into bourgeois democratic revolution, established the Restoration Society and joined in the United Allegiance Society, ever served as the first Minister of Education of the Provisional Government of the Republic of China. In January 1917, he assumed the post of chancellor of Peking University ("Beida") and implemented the principle of running a university known as "all-embracing openness to ideas and freedom of thought". He reformed Beida, turned the decadent old Beida into a modern university that was thriving, robust and active in thinking, and made it the center of New Culture Movement and the origin of May 4th Patriotic Movement. Later on, he acted as a standing committee of Republican Government, the head of graduate department, the president of Academia Sinica, and initiated and organized China League for Civil Rights. Mr. Cai Yuanpei died of illness in Hong Kong on March 5, 1940.

周作人曾评价说："蔡子民的主要成就，是在他的改革北大。"沈尹默甚至极而言之："纵观蔡先生一生，也只有在北大的那几年留下了成绩。"而蔡元培在执掌北大校务的几年中，特别是五四运动期间主要工作生活在东堂子胡同75号院。做过北大旁听生的孙伏园曾感叹说："五四运动的历史意义，一年比一年更趋明显；五四运动的具体印象，却一年比一年更趋淡忘了。"现在，我们只能通过追寻蔡元培及其同时代人的回忆片段，大致连缀出蔡元培当年在北

京生活的真实场景和人际交往，领悟一个文化领袖在乱世危情中的泰然襟怀。

Zhou Zuoren ever commented him as "The main achievement of Cai Jiemin lies in his reform of Beida." Shen Yinmo even said in an extreme manner, "Looking at Mr. Cai's life, his achievements were only found in these few years when he was working in Peking University." Cai Yuanpei mainly worked and lived in No. 75 Yard of Dongtangzi Alley during the years when he took charge of administrative affairs of Beida, in particular during the May 4th Movement Period. Sun Fuyuan, a guest student of Beida ever, said with a sigh, "The historical significance of May 4th Movement is becoming increasingly evident year by year, but the specific impression of May 4th Movement is fading into oblivion year by year". Now, we can only patch up the true scenes and personal associations of Cai Yuanpei when he lived in Beijing and understand the broad bosom of a great cultural leader in a turbulent age through tracing the fragmental memories of Cai Yuanpei and his contemporaries.

蔡元培（左三）出席中华民国临时政府第一次国务会议（上图）
Cai Yuanpei (the third from left) participated in the first cabinet conference of the Nanjing Provisional Government (the upper picture)
袁世凯内阁成员合影，前排左一为教育总长蔡元培（下图）
A photo of Yuan Shikai cabinet. Cai Yuanpei as Minister of Education was in the front row, first from the left. (the lower picture)

1916年9月1日，身在法国巴黎的蔡元培收到北洋政府教育总长范源濂的电报，电云："国事渐平，教育宜急。现以首都最高学府尤赖大贤主宰，师表群伦，海内人士咸深景仰。用特专电敦请我公担任北京大学校长一席，务祈鉴允，早日归国，以慰瞻望。"后来范源廉自述："蔡先生很伟大。他到北大作校长，是我作教育部长时，民五冬天从欧洲请回的。民国元年，我到教育部作次长，却是他邀请的，我和他是肝胆相照的朋友。"

On September 1, 1916, Cai Yuanpei who was then in Paris

of France, received a telegram from Fan Yuanlian, the Minister of Education of Beiyang Government, saying "The situation in the country has become calmer and the need for education is urgent. Presently the highest school in the capital needs the leadership of a worthy man who can set an example for the people to follow. Our public figures hold you in the highest esteem. We earnestly hope that you will accept the chancellorship at Peking University and return to the country at the earliest hour." Fan Yuanlian later accounted himself, "Mr. Cai is a great man. He was invited back from Europe to be the chancellor of Peking University on the 5th year of Republic of China when I was the Education Minister. I took the post of Vice Minister of Education on the 1st year of ROC upon the invitation by him. We are friends frank and true to each other."

蔡元培担任中华民国临时政府教育总长的委任状
The certificate of appointment of Cai Yuanpei served as provisional Republic's Minister of Education

北京大学呈大总统报明蔡元培到校任职的公函
The inaugural letter submitted to president by Peking University

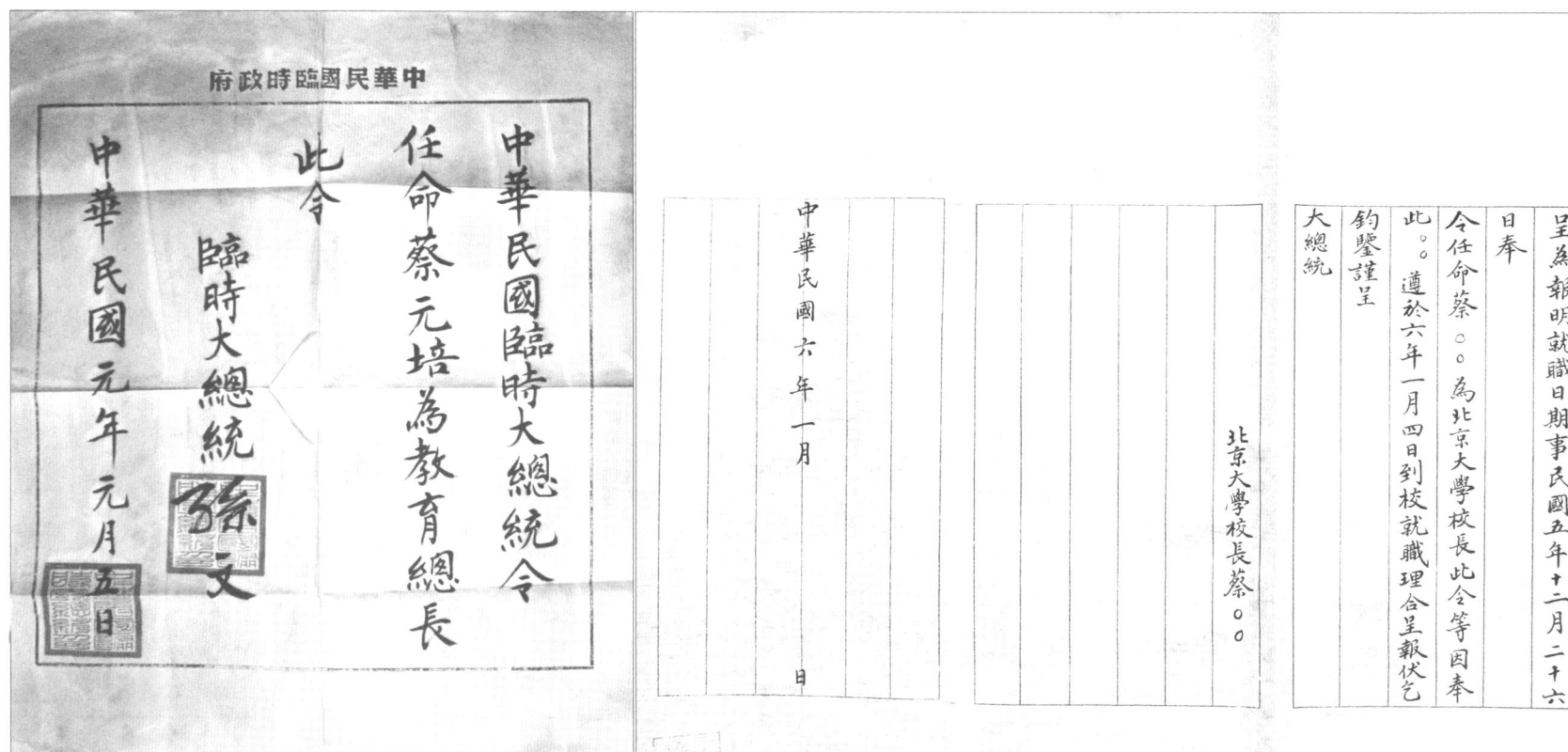

收到这封恳请自己回国出任北大校长的电报，蔡元培思忖良久，心潮起伏，一时难以平静下来。清翰林出身、后为忠诚的革命党人的蔡元培，早在15年前就走上了民主革命、教育救国的道路。他以年近5旬之身去国远游，留学法国，其目的就是要融合中西文化，培养硕学闳材，以教育救国强国。在法国，他和吴玉章等发起勤工俭学会和华法教育会，努力为中国有志青年赴法勤工俭学创造条件。留法勤工俭学在当时国内进步知识分子中产生很大影响，不少人积极参加到这一行列中来，其中一些人在法国开始接受马克思主义教育，逐步成长为马克思主义者和中国共产党的优秀领导人。虽然留法勤工俭学取得了进展，但蔡元培并不满意。他总觉得"在国外经营之教育，又似不及在国内之切实"。现在机会来了，擅权专制的袁世凯倒台了，国家出现了新的转机和希望。尽管当时北京大学的风气口碑不好，但它毕竟是由中央政府举办的中国第一所国立大学，是对全国教育有举足轻重影响的最高学府，他可以把北大作为基地，施展自己的抱负，实现自己的夙愿。经过一番考虑，蔡元培初步打算接受范源濂的邀请，回国出任北大校长。

After receiving the telegram sincerely inviting him back to accept the chancellorship of Beida, Cai Yuanpei thought for a long time with stirring emotions and could not calm himself down for a while. Cai Yuanpei, who was originally a member of the Hanlin Academy and became later a devoted revolutionist, embarked on the road of democratic revolution and "saving the country by promoting education" as early as 15 years ago. At the age of nearly fifty, he went abroad alone and studied in France, with an aim to integrate Chinese and Western culture, train great talents and save and strengthen the country with education. In France, he

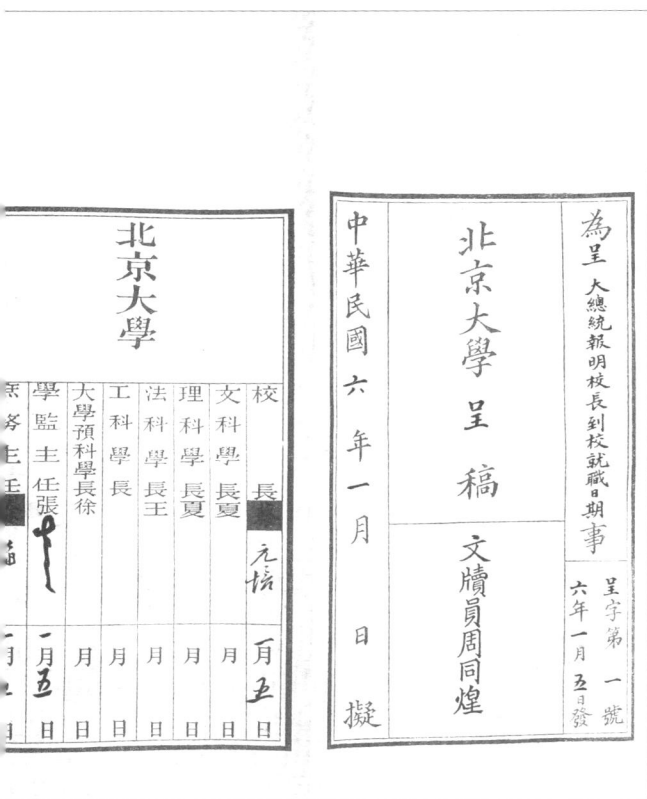

and Wu Yuzhang initiated Work-study Society and Societe Franco-Chinoise d' Education and made efforts to create work opportunities for ambitious young Chinese to study in France. The work-study program in France produced substantial impact among the progressive intellectuals at home then, and many of them joined in this rank actively. Some intellectuals began to receive Marxist education in France and grew gradually into Marxists and outstanding CCP leaders. Despite the progresses made in the work-study program, Cai Yuanpei was not satisfied. He always felt that to run education in a foreign country was not so practical as at home. Now the opportunity came. The autocratic Yuan Shikai was toppled and the republic turned up new turns and hopes. In spite of its bad styles and reputation then, after all, Beida was the first state university of China founded by the central government and was the highest school being a crucial part in the education of the country. Using Beida as the base, he could make his aspirations and wishes come true. Thinking it over, Cai Yuanpei had an initial plan to accept the invitation of Fan Yuanlian to be the chancellor of Beida.

一个月后的1916年10月2日，蔡元培同吴玉章一道由马赛乘船回国，11月8日抵达上海。对于蔡元培是否出任北大校长一事，在他的友人中有不同看法，在一些革命党人中也有异议。不少人劝他不要进北大这个是非之地，弄不好反倒会坏了自己的名声。对蔡元培深有所知的孙中山却主张他去，认为像蔡元培这样的老同志应当去那历代帝王

蔡元培担任北京大学校长的任命状
The President of the Republic of China, Li Yuanhong signing the commission appointing Cai Yuanpei as the president of Peking University

和官僚气氛笼罩下的北京，主持全国性教育，传播革命思想。孙中山的支持和嘱托坚定了蔡元培任职北大、改造北大的决心。他当时曾说："觉北京大学虽声名狼藉，然改良之策，亦未尝不可一试，故允为担任。"后来还用"我不入地狱谁入地狱"这句话表示自己毅然决然的态度。1916年12月22日，蔡元培抱着整顿、改革北大的宗旨和决心，迎难而上，赴京就任北大校长的职务。

One month later, on October 2, 1916, Cai Yuanpei and Wu Yuzhang came back home by boat from Marseilles and arrived in Shanghai on November 8. Regarding whether he should take the post of chancellor of Beida or not, his friends held different opinions, so did his revolutionary colleagues. Many persuaded him not to enter Beida, a troublesome place, lest it would tarnish his good reputation. But Sun Yat-Sen who knew Cai Yuanpei well urged him to take the chance. Sun believed that an old comrade like Cai Yuanpei should go to Beijing shrouded in past emperors and bureaucratic atmosphere to take charge of national education and disseminate revolutionary spirit. The support and trust from Sun Yat-sen confirmed Cai Yuanpei's resolution to work in and reform Beida. He ever said then, "Though Peking University is now infamous, we can still try the proposal of reform, so please allow me to take the post." Later he also revealed his firm resolution with the quotation "If someone has to take the tough task, let me do it". On December 22, 1916, cherishing the tenet and resolution of "straightening out and reforming Beida", he went to Beijing and assumed the post of chancellor of Beida against all difficulties.

思想自由 兼容并包

1916年12月26日，蔡元培正式被任命为北京大学校长。1917年1月4日，蔡元培到北大就职视事，从此开始了他一生中最有成就也最为人所景仰的一段辉煌历程。既有革新精神又有民主作风的蔡元培，从踏进北大校门的那一刻起就与他的前任截然不同。他到校的第一天，校工们排队在校门口恭恭敬敬地向他行礼。他一反以前历任校长目中无人、不予理睬的惯例，脱下礼帽郑重其事地向校工们鞠躬回礼。此后，他每天出入校门，校警向他致敬，他都脱帽还礼。这一件令校工和学生感到惊讶的新鲜事，不啻是给封建积习严重的北大人吹进一股强劲的平等民主之风，预示着这所学校将在改革中走上新的途程。

Cai Yuanpei was formally appointed as the chancellor of Beida on December 26, 1916. On January 4, 1917, Cai Yuanpei came to Beida and assumed office, thus began a splendid period in his life which is the most fruitful in results and mostly admired by people. With both reformative spirit and democratic style, Cai Yuanpei proved himself different from his predecessors at the moment he stepped into the gate of Beida. On the first day of his arrival, the faculty queued at the gate to welcome him respectfully. In contrary to his haughty and arrogant predecessors, he removed his hat and reciprocated their bows. Afterwards, the guard would salute him whenever he passed by the gate, every time he would take off his hat and return the respect. That was astonishing news to the university faculty and students and is really strong wind of equality and democracy blown into Beida which was then shrouded in heavy feudal atmosphere. It was an indication that this school would embark on a new course in the reform.

这是蔡元培第七次来到北京。他原本对北京南城的房子情有独钟，在供职翰林院做京官时，曾借住过南城绳匠胡同的同乡李慈铭寓所和南半截胡同绍兴县馆。这次到京后最初租居南城官菜园上街陈宅，旋迁东城遂安伯胡同4号（后转作华法教育会临时办事处）；随后又租住东堂子胡同75号院的房子。东堂子胡同75号，旧时的门牌是东堂子胡同

北京大学第一院（北大红楼）
The No. 1 Courtyard of Peking University ("Red Tower")

33号，在胡同西段北侧，是一座坐北朝南的三进院落。蔡元培寓此时，将一进院的5间南房（俗称倒座房）安置仆人和门房。二进院3间北房为蔡元培的孩子居住，前有走廊，左右各带1间耳房作厨房和储藏间，东、西厢房各3间为亲友客房，南房4间作为会客的客厅，第三进北房5间为蔡元培的卧室和书房，带走廊。当时北京房屋的租赁价格并不高，平均下来每间房每月租金一块大洋（如胡适1918年租赁的钟鼓寺14号院共有17间房屋，房租每月20银元），以北大校长每月600大洋的收入，花费区区20多块银元租个小院似乎与蔡元培身份不符。推测其原因是，当时并未马上弃租遂安伯胡同4号院，因故就近在其南侧东堂子胡同择宅，方便往来罢了。因为距离沙滩大街的北京大学很近，东堂子胡同蔡寓便成为蔡元培平日校外会客、工作和休息的主要场所，直到1921年因蔡元培夫人黄仲玉不幸病故，旧宅难免睹物伤情，这才租赁西单背阴胡同的房产安置新家。

It was Cai's seventh time to Beijing. He showed special preference to the houses in southern Beijing at first, when he was a capital official in Hanlin Imperial Academy, he ever rent the house of his countryman Li Ciming located at Shengjiang Alley of southern Beijing and Shaoxing County Residence of Nanbanjie Alley. After he arrived in Beijing this time, he rent the Chen Family's house at Guancaiyuan Upper Street of Southern Beijing at first, and later moved to No. 4 of Suianbo Alley of Dongcheng District (later changed into the temporary office of Societe Franco-Chinoise d'Education); afterwards he rent the house of No. 75 yard of Dongtangzi Alley. No.75 of Dongtangzi alley, whose doorplate was No.33 before, located at the north side of the west section of the alley, is a south-facing triple courtyard. When residing there,

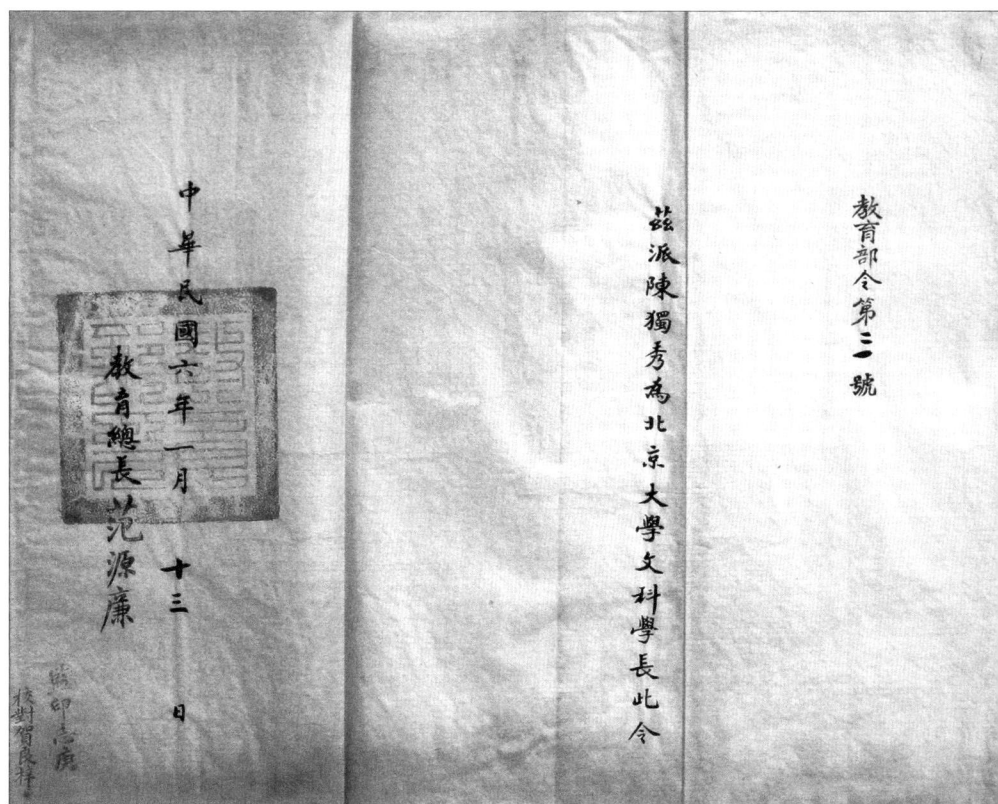

教育部令第三號

茲派陳獨秀為北京大學文科學長此令

中華民國六年一月 十三 日
教育總長范源廉

Cai Yuanpei assigned the 5 south-facing rooms (nicknamed as reverse seat) of the first courtyard for servants and doormen. The 3 south-facing rooms of the 2nd courtyard were residence of Cai Yuanpei's children, with a corridor in front. There was a side room on each side as the kitchen and storehouse, the wing rooms, three on each side, were guestrooms for relatives and friends, the 4 north-facing rooms were the living room for receiving guests. The 5 south-facing rooms of the 3rd courtyard with a corridor were the bedroom and study of Cai Yuanpei. The rent was not high in Beijing at that time with each room costs 1 silver dollar each month on average (for example, the No.14 yard at Zhonggusi rent by Hu Shi in 1918 included 17 rooms, the total rent was 20 silver dollars each month). As the chancellor of Beida whose monthly income was as high as 600 silver dollars, it seemed quite unfit for him to rent such a small courtyard with only 20 silver dollars. The speculated reason is that because he didn't give up renting No. 4 courtyard of Suianbo Alley immediately so he chose

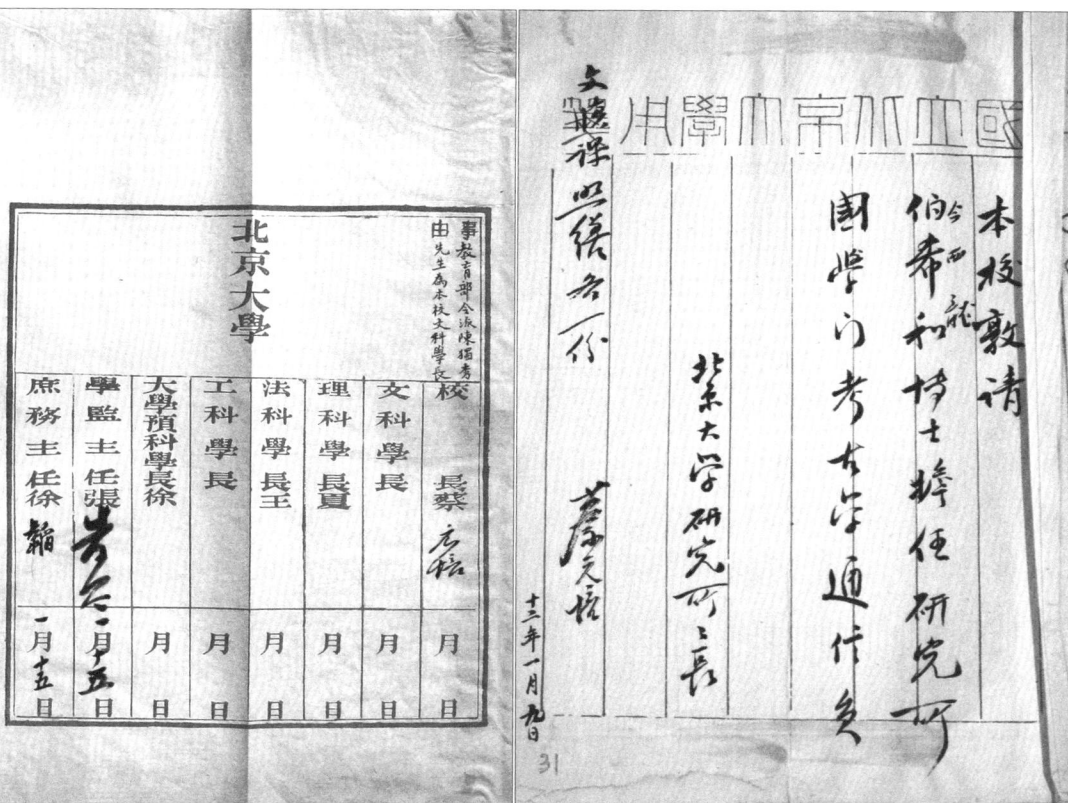

教育部派陈独秀为北京大学文科学长令（左图）
The order of Ministry of Education appointed Chen Duxiu as the Dean of Arts in Peking University. (the left picture)
聘请法国著名汉学家保罗伯希和担任北京大学国学门考古学通行员的公函（右图）
The official letter employed Paul Pelliot, famous French sinologist, as the messenger of archaeology in the Chinese National Culture College of Peking University. (the right picture)

a house nearby in its south side at Dongtangzi alley just for convenient commute. As very close to Beida on Shatan Street, the residence of Cai Yuanpei in Dongtangzi Alley had been a main place for him to receive guests, work and rest outside Beida, until the unfortunate death of his wife Huang Zhongyu in 1921. At the sight of the old house and familiar things, he could not help but being heart-broken, he then rent a house of Beiyin Alley of Xidan as his new residence.

此后，蔡元培在北京大学兴利除弊，祛旧布新，使陈腐的北大一变而为鲜活的北大，名副其实的北大。蔡元培在《我在北京大学的经历》中记述："我到京后，先访医专校长汤尔和君，问北大情形。他说：'文科预科的情形，可问沈尹默君；理工科的情形，可问夏浮筠君。'汤君又说：'文科学长如未定，可请陈仲甫君；陈君现改名独秀，主编《新青年》杂志，确可为青年的指导者。'因取《新青年》十余本示我。我对于陈君，本来有一种不忘的印象，就是我与刘申叔君同在《警钟日报》服务时，刘君语我：'有一种在芜湖发行之白话报，发起的若干人，都因困苦及危险而散去了，陈仲甫一个人又支持了好几个月。'现在听汤君的话，又翻阅了《新青年》，决意聘他。从汤君处探知陈君寓在前门外一旅馆，我即往访，与之订定。于是陈君来北大任文科学长，而夏君原任理科学长，沈君亦原任教授，一仍旧贯。乃相与商定整顿北大的办法，次第执行。"

Afterward, Cai Yuanpei promoted the beneficial and eliminated the harmful, pushed out the old and ushered in the new, turned the stale Beida into a vigorous and authentic one. Cai Yuanpei related in his "My Experience in Peking University", "When arrived in Beijing, I first called on Mr. Tang Erhe, the president of Medical College, and inquired him of the situations of Beida. He told me to consult Shen Yinmo about preparatory humanities,

蔡元培（左二）与蒋梦麟（左一）、胡适（左三）、李大钊（右一）的合影
The group photo of Cai Yuanpei (the second from left), Jiang Menglin (the first from left), Hu Shi (the third from left) and Li Dazhao (the first from right)

《新青年》三卷六号
The New Youth Journal, volume 3, No. 6

and Xia Fujun about science and engineering. Tang added that if the dean of humanities had not been decided, I should invite Chen Zhongfu; he was renamed as Chen Duxiu then, was the chief editor of *New Youth*, and could be indeed the instructor of youth. He then showed me a dozen copies of *New Youth*. As to Chen, I had already an unforgettable impression. It was when I served for *Alarming Bell Daily* together with Liu Shenshu, I was told by him that there was a newspaper in plain language distributed in Wuhu; almost all the initiators dispersed due to difficulties and danger, Chen Zhongfu alone supported for another several months. I decided to recruit him after hearing Tang's words and looking through *New Youth*. I knew from Tang that Chen was living in a hotel at Qianmenwai, I went to visit him immediately and after meeting we come to an agreement on recruitment. Therefore, Chen came to serve as the Dean of Humanities and Xia Junyuan Dean of Science, Shen Junyi a professor as usual. I then discussed with them the measures to reform Beida and implemented those measures in order"

据与陈独秀同住旅馆的《新青年》承销商汪孟邹在日记中写道："蔡先生差不多天天要来看仲甫。"有时候蔡元培来得早，陈独秀还没起，他就"招呼茶房，不要叫醒，只要拿凳子给他坐在门口等候"。陈独秀最初不想受聘北大文科学长，说要回上海办《新青年》。蔡元培劝他把《新青年》搬到北京来办，他才答应就任。陈独秀曾担心："我从没在大学教过书，又没有什么学位头衔，能否胜任，不得而知。"蔡元培竟为陈独秀杜撰了一套假履历。在《致教育部请派文科学长》的公函中，他虚构陈独秀是"日本东京大学毕业，曾任芜湖安徽公学教务长、安徽高等学校校长"。为了推举陈独秀出任北大文科领军之人，蔡元培可谓用心良苦，甚至使用了不同寻常的手段。

As Wang Mengzou, the underwriter of *New Youth* who lived in the same hotel as Chen Duxiu did, wrote in his dairy, "Mr. Cai came to see Zhongfu almost every day." Sometimes, Cai Yuanpei came early while Chen Duxiu was still in bed. He then told the waiter not to awaken him and just bring a stool for him to wait at the door. At first, Chen Duxiu didn't want to assume the position of dean of humanities of Beida and said he would go back to Shanghai to run the *New Youth*. Cai Yuanpei persuaded him to move *New Youth* to Beijing, he then agreed to assume the post. Chen Duxiu was ever worried that whether he would be qualified since he never taught in university nor did he possess any academic titles. Out of Chen's imagination, Cai Yuanpei worked out a fake resume for him! In the official letter "Petition to Ministry of Education for Assigning Dean of Humanities", he fabricated that Chen Duxiu was graduated from Tokyo University of Japan, ever worked as Anhui Academic Dean of Wuhu and president of Anhui Higher Learning School. In order to recommend Chen Duxiu to be one of the leaders of humanities of Beida, Cai Yuanpei paid well-meaning efforts indeed and even applied unusual measures.

蔡元培还亲自前往北大译学馆看望有"鬼谷子"之称的沈尹默教授。沈尹默在回访时也向蔡元培推荐陈独秀任北大文科学长，提出："我建议您向政府提出三点要求：第一，北大经费要有保障；第二，北大的章程上规定教师组织评议会，而教育部始终不许成立。中国有句古话：百足之虫，死而不僵。与其集大权于一身，不如把大权交给教授，教授治校，这样，将来即使你走了，学校也不会乱。因此我主张您力争根据章程，成立评议会；第三，规定每隔一定年限，派教员和学生到外国留学。"蔡元培深以为然，完全采纳。后来蔡元培在校内事务上多问计于沈尹默，沈尹默一度出任文科学长。

Cai Yuanpei also went to the Translation Institute of Beida in person to see Prof. Shen Yinmo, who had a nickname of "Guiguzi", an ancient master of politics, diplomacy, military strategy and fortune-telling. When a returning visit, Shen Yinmo also recommended to Cai Yuanpei that Chen Duxiu should be the dean of Humanities of Beida, saying "I advice you to propose three requirements to the government: 1. The finance of Beida shall be guaranteed; 2. The constitution of Beida shall provide that teachers are to organize a policy-making council, but the Ministry of Education has been disapproving its establishment. There is an old saying in China: a centipede dies but never falls down. You would rather hand out the power to professors instead of having the great power within your hand and let the professors govern the school. In this way, the school will not become disordered even when you leave in the future. Therefore, I hold that you shall strive to establish the council according to the constitution; 3. It shall be provided that teachers and students shall be sent abroad to study at regular interval of years." Cai Yuanpei totally agreed and took all his advices. Later on, Cai Yuanpei frequently consulted Shen Yinmo about school matters and Shen Yinmo ever holding the post of dean of humanities.

要推动北京大学的教育制度改革，必须先要得到教师中坚力量的支持。蔡元培依靠前清翰林和前教育总长的资历、自身人格信念的感召力和北京大学浙江籍同乡的地缘人脉关系，在短期内确立了校长权威，重组新型教授团队。他相继聘请了胡适、李大钊、钱玄同、刘半农、吴虞、鲁迅、周作人等具有革新思想和丰博学识的新派人物到北大文科任教。此外，马叙伦、沈尹默、陈垣、陈大齐、萧友梅、沈兼士、徐悲鸿、熊十力、马寅初、陶孟和、王世杰、周鲠生、陈启修、高一涵等国内知名专家学者，也被聘为北大文科、法科教授、导师。在理工科方面．蔡元培聘请当时国内第一个介绍爱因斯坦相对论的物理学家夏元瑮担任理科学长，还聘请知名学者李四光、丁燮林、颜任光、何杰、翁文灏、王星拱、李书华、丁文江、俞同奎、朱家骅、冯祖荀、秦汾以及

著名画家沈嘉蔚的油画《北大钟声》，描绘了蔡元培做校长时期的北京大学，真正意义上的兼容和宽容。画中共16人，由左至右是：刘师培、黄侃、沈尹默、陈独秀、胡适、朱希祖、辜鸿铭、马叙伦、蔡元培、李大钊、马幼渔、鲁迅、周作人、钱玄同、梁漱溟、刘半农
The painting, the *Bell of Peking University* by Shen Jiawei, a famous painter, depicted the really atmosphere of absorbing and tolerance when Cai Yuanpei as the chancellor of Peking University.

外籍专家葛利普等为教授。一时间，北大名师荟萃，人才济济，学术空气浓厚活跃，教学科研盛况空前。据1918年初的统计，全校共有教授90名，从其中76名的年龄来看，35岁以下者43名，占56.6％；50岁以上者仅6名，占7.9％；最年轻的教授徐宝璜只有21岁；胡适、刘半农也只有二十七八岁；陈独秀也才38岁。这样年轻而富于活力的教师队伍，一扫北大过去的陈腐之气，使北大成为鲁迅所说的"常为新的改进的运动的先锋"。

To promote the reform of education system of Beida, gaining support of the backbone of the faculty is essential. In virtue of his identity of Hanli scholar of the former Qing dynasty, his qualification as the former minister of education, the charisma of his own personality and faith and the geographic and personal relations with his countrymen in Beida, within a short period of time, he established his authority as the chancellor and reorganized a new team of professors. He recruited in succession new school persons with reformative thinking and rich knowledge to teach in humanities division of Beida, such persons include Hu Shi, Li Dazhao, Qian Xuantong, Liu Bannong, Wu Yu, Lu Xun and Zhou Zuoren, etc. In addition, famous domestic experts and scholars like Ma Xulun, Shen Yinmo, Chen Yuan, Chen Daqi, Xiao Youmei, Shen Jianshi, Xu Beihong, Xiong Shili, Ma Yinchu, Tao Menghe, Wang Shijie, Zhou Gengsheng, Chen Qixiu and Gao Yihan, were also invited to assume positions of professors and tutors of humanities division, school of laws. Cai Yuanpie also recruited physicist Xia Yuanli, the first person in China to introduce the theory of relativity of Einstein, to assume the position of dean of school of science and engineering; he also invited famous scholars like Li Siguang, Ding Xielin, Yan Renguang, He Jie, Weng Wenhao, Wang Xinggong, Li Shuhua, Ding Wenjiang, Yu Tongkui, Zhu Jiahua, Feng Zugou, Qin Fen and foreign expert Grabau, to be professors. At a time, there was a big host of famous teachers and an abundance of capable people in Beida, its academic atmosphere was strong and active, it's pomp of teaching and research was unprecedented. According to the statistics of early 1918, Beida had a total of 90 professors. Judging from the age of the 76 professors, there were 43 professors aged below 35, taking up 56.6%; there were only 6 professors whose age were above 50, accounting for 7.9%. The youngest professor Xu Baohuang was as young as 21, Hu Shi and Liu Bannong were only about 27 or 28. Chen Duxiu was only 38 years old. Such a young and vibrant faculty team swept across the decadent atmosphere of Beida and made Beida "a pioneer of new progressive movements" as described by Lu Xun.

蔡元培在国内延聘名师，不问派别，不问师从，甚至不问学历，但求其术有专攻，学有专长。例如将仅有高中学历、24岁的梁漱溟聘为讲师，后又聘为教授，主讲《印度哲学》。又如，蔡元培想请王国维到北大教书。但王国维以清朝遗老自居，不能为民国做事，坚决不答应。蔡元培无奈之下想了个变通的办法，让他做通信导师（类似今天函授教授），为北大教学生，名义上却不是北大教师。蔡元培令人送去200元的工资，王国维却无论如何不肯收，因为他觉得虽为北大做事，但毕竟未受聘于北大，就不能拿工资。最后蔡元培又是变通了一下，以报销通信教授邮费的名义，才让贫困中的王国维收下了这笔钱。

Cai Yuanpei recruited renowned teachers at home regardless of their cliques, teachers and even their academic degrees, but valued only their specialties. For example, he recruited 24-year-old Liang Shuming who was graduated from high school as lecturer and later professor to teach *Indian Philosophy*. Another example, Cai

1918年8月，北京大学红楼建成，是北大文科、校部、图书馆所在地
"Red Tower" was built up as the place where there were the Arts Department, school office and library in August 1918

Yuanpei wanted to recruit Wang Guowei to teach at Beida. However, Wang Guowei, claiming himself an old adherent of Qing Dynasty, turned down the invitation resolutely, saying that he could not work for the republic. To be flexible, Cai Yuanpei asked Wang Guowei to be the correspondence director (similar to correspondence professor today) and teach students of Beida, but he was not a teacher of Beida in name. Cai Yuanpei asked others to send 200 silver dollars to Wang Guowei as his salary, but Wang Guowei refused to take it anyway as he thought that though he worked for Beida, he was not recruited by it, so he could not get the payment. At last, Cai Yuanpei worked out a flexible way again and managed to make Wang Guowei in poverty accept the money in the name of reimbursement of postage of correspondence professor.

蔡元培为北大聘请了美国地质学教授葛利普等外籍教授，并邀请著名学者英国哲学家罗素、美国教育家杜威、法国数学家班乐卫等来校讲学。至于不合格的教员，蔡元培坚决黜退，不管对方是什么来头，有什么靠山。蔡元培为辞退北大不称职的外籍教员曾屡遭外交部质问。一位被辞退的英国教员搬出英国驻华公使朱尔典来谈判，蔡元培不肯妥协。朱尔典悻悻而归说："蔡元培是不要再做校长的了！"被辞退的外籍教授告到法庭，蔡元培请北大兼职讲师、曾任司法总长的王宠惠作代理人，最后校方胜诉。

北京大学授予班乐卫和芮恩施名誉博士学位
Paul Painlevè and Reinsch were granted the honorary doctorate by Peking University.

Cai Yuanpei recruited foreign professors such as professor of geology Grabau from the U.S., and invited famous scholars such as British philosopher Roseau, US educator Dewey and French mathematician Painleve to lecture in Beida. For faculty members who are not qualified, Cai Yuanpei dismissed them with resolution, no matter what was their background or backing. Cai Yuanpei was ever frequently interrogated by Ministry of Foreign Affairs for dismissing unqualified foreign teachers. A dismissed British teacher turned to Jordan, the ambassador of U.K to China, for negotiation, but Cai Yuanpei didn't not compromise. Jordan returned resentfully, saying "Cai Yuanpei's term is ending!" The dismissed foreign professor filed a lawsuit to court, Cai Yuanpei asked Wang Chonghui, a part-time lecturer of Beida and the former minister of judicature, as his procurator, Beida won the case finally.

北京大学内反对新文化运动的国学教授黄侃说："余与蔡子民志不同，道不合，然蔡去，余亦决不愿留，因环顾中国，除蔡子民外，亦无能用余之人。"另一个保守派、留着长辫子的辜鸿铭在课堂上对学生们讲："中国只有两个好人，一个是蔡元培先生，

北京大学实行评议制度，由教授选出的评议会是全校最高权力机构。这是1919年北京大学评议会选举结果（上图）
Peking University implemented appraisal system and appraisal meeting which was selected by professors as the high authority. This is the results selected by appraisal meeting of Peking University in 1919. (the upper picture)

北京大学汇聚不同政治倾向和不同学派的学者，开创了学术自由、思想自由的一代新风。这是刊登《北京大学日刊》上的1918年《文本科第二学期课程表》（下图）
The scholars with different political inclination and different schools were gathered in Peking University and the new fashion freedom of academic and thinking were created. This is the curriculum of arts in second semester published in *Peking University Daily* in 1918. (the lower picture)

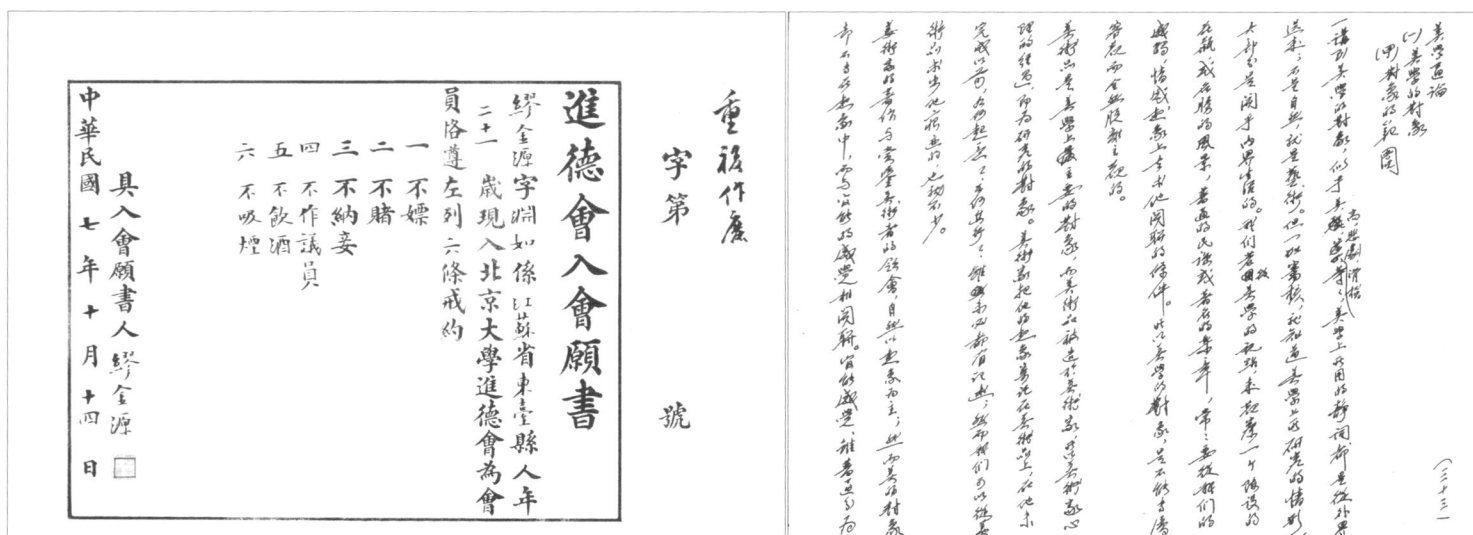

1918年6月，蔡元培发起成立进德会。这是北大学生缪金源的进德会入会愿书
Cai Yuanpei organized and founded Jindehui in June 1918. This is the
application of Miu Jinyuan, a student of Peking University

蔡元培撰写《美学通论》手稿
The manuscript of *General Aesthetics*
compiled by Cai Yuanpei

一个是我。"陈独秀称赞蔡元培道："这样容纳异己的雅量，尊重学术自由思想的卓见，在习于专制、好同恶异的东方人中实所罕有。"胡适则评论说："蔡公是真能做领袖的。他自己学问上的成绩，思想上的地位，都不算高。但他能充分用人，他用人的成绩都可算是他的成绩。"胡适还在1935年7月26日致罗隆基信中说："蔡先生能充分信用他手下的人，每委人一事，他即付以全权，不再过问，遇有困难时，他却挺身负其全责，若有成功，他每啧啧归功于主任的人，然而外人每归功于他老人家。因此，人每乐为之用，又乐为尽力。迹近于无为，而实则尽人之才，此是做领袖的绝大本领。"梁漱溟深有感慨地说："蔡先生的了不起，首先是他能认识人，使用人，维护人。用人得当，各尽其才，使每个人都能发出自己的热和光，这力量可就大了。"

 Huang Kan, a professor of traditional sinology in Beida who objected the new culture movement, said, "I am different from Cai Jiemin and we are following different paths. However, since Cai has left, I am determined not to stay. As looking around China, there is no one else who can order me except Cai." Another conservative, Gu Hongming with a long pigtail, told his students in class, "There are only two good men in China. One is Mr. Cai Yuanpei, the other one is me." Chen Duxiu praised Cai Yuanpei as "Such a grace of tolerating dissidents and a remarkable insight of respect for free academic thought is really rare among orientals who are accustomed to dictation, fond of men with same mind but loathe dissidents." Hu Shi commented, "Mr. Cai can be a real

北京大学文科英文学门第一次毕业班师生合影（前排左三为蔡元培）
The first group photo of teachers and students in English College of Peking University.
(Cai Yuanpei was in the front row, third from the left)

leader. Neither his academic achievements nor his spiritual level is that high. But he is a master in allocating appropriate duty to different people, his achievements in making use of personnel can also be counted as his achievements." On July 26, 1935, Hu Shi also said in his letter to Luo Longji, "Mr. Cai can have full trust in his subordinates. If he entrust something to a person, he will give him or her the full authority and will not ask again. If difficulties arise, he will stand out to shoulder all responsibilities. In case of success, he will praise the person-in-charge. However, others will accredit the success to him. Therefore, people are glad to work for him and exert their efforts. He seemed inactive but actually made the most of people's talents, this is the greatest ability of a leader". Liang Shuming sighed with deep emotion, "The greatness of Mr. Cai lies in first his sharp eyes for discovering competent people, his ability of using and defending people. Therefore, he can make proper and best use of talents. As a result, everyone can contribute their own efforts. Such strength then becomes very powerful. "

蔡元培早在1913年即有意出任北大校长，只是由于袁世凯的反对，未能如愿。他对北大教学体制改革早已胸有成竹。他说："现在是国家教育创制的开始，要撇开个人的偏见、党派的立场，给教育立一个统一的智慧的百年大计。""人言有良社会斯有良大学，吾谓有良大学斯有良社会。"蔡元培主张"教育独立"的思想。他在《教育独立议》一文中指出："教育是帮助被教育的人，给他能发展自己的能力，完成他的人格，于人类文化上能尽一分子的责任；不是把被教育的人，造成一种特别器具，给抱有他种目的的人去应用的。所以，教育事业当完全交与教育家，保有独立的资格，毫不受各派政党或各派教会的影响。"

As early as 1913, Cai Yuanpei had the intention to serve as chancellor of Beida, but failed due to the objection of Yuan Shikai. He had cherished a well-shaped plan for the reform of educational system of Beida long before. He said, "It is the beginning of education innovation of the country now, we shall set aside personal prejudice and standpoints of different parties, so as to establish a uniform and wise 100-year plan for education." "People said that conscientious universities came out of a conscientious society, but I think a conscientious society comes out of a conscientious university." Cai Yuanpei upheld the idea of "independent education". He pointed out in his "Argument on Independent Education", "Education is to help the educated, bestow them the ability to develop themselves, consummate their characters and make them play their own part in human culture; it is not to forge them into special tools for the use of people with other purposes. Therefore, the cause of education shall be all entrusted to educators and keep its independent status, not subject to any influence from various parties or education organizations."

1917年1月9日，北京大学举行开学典礼。蔡元培发表演说，对学生提出三点要求：一曰抱定宗旨，为求学而来；二曰砥砺德行，责无旁贷；三曰敬爱师友，以诚相待。他开宗明义地宣称："大学学生，当以研究学术为天职，不当以大学为升官发财之阶梯。"随即，蔡元培发表公告："以后学生对校长应用公函，不得再用呈文。"锐意革除北大的官衔作风。不久便提出并实施"囊括大典，网罗众家，思想自由，兼容并包"的办学方针。蔡元培还引经据典解释说："我在北大实行'思想自由，兼容并包'，这可以用《礼记·中庸》里的话来说明，那就是'万物并育而不相害，道并行而不相悖'"。

Beida held its opening ceremony on January 9, 1917. Cai Yuanpei delivered a speech, putting forward three requirements for the students: 1. They shall hold fast to their tenet, i.e. they came to Beida for learning; 2. It is their unshakable responsibility to cultivate their morals and ethics; 3. They shall respect and love teachers and friends and be frank to each other. He proclaimed openly, "University students shall take academic research as their holy duty other than as the ladder toward office and wealth. Briefly afterwards, Cai Yuanpei published a bulletin "Students shall present official letters to the president and shall no longer use petitions" to reform the bureaucratic style of Beida

北京大学文科国文门第四次毕业班师生合影
（前排左三为蔡元培）（左图）
The fourth group photo of teachers and students in the
Chinese National Culture College of Peking University. (Cai
Yuanpei was in the front row, third from the left) (the left
picture)
1917年6月，蔡元培与北京大学中国哲学门第一届毕业班师生留影
（前排右四为陈独秀、右五蔡元培）（右图）
A group photo of Cai Yuanpei and the teachers and students
from the first graduating class in Philosophy College of Peking
University in June 1917. (Chen Duxiu was in the front row,
fourth from the right; Cai Yuanpei was in the front row, fifth
from the right) (the right picture)

determinedly. Soon he proposed and carried out the principle
of running a school known as "Inclusion of Great Classics,
Concentration of Various Experts, Freedom of Thoughts, an All-
bracing Openness to Ideas". Cai Yuanpei also made an illustration
by quoting classics, saying "My adoption of the principle of
freedom of thought and an all-embracing doctrine can be
explained by words from *Middle of the Road of Book of Rites*,
i.e. 'all things on earth grow together without one doing harm to
another and all doctrines in the world develop in parallel with
each other without coming into conflict' ".

北京大学教学体制改革的核心主旨是学术至上、教授治校。蔡
元培主张学与术分校，文与理通科。在胡适的建议下，将"学
年制"改为"学分制"，实行"选科制"。调动学生学习的积极性、
主动性，以利于因材施教。关于选科的确定，分别由本科和预
科教授会负责，对于一年级新生，专门设立新生指导委员会作

为其入学选课的顾问。选科制于1919年在北大首先实行，1922年起全国其他大学也陆续采用。学校成立学术研究所，推进学术独立；创办消费公社和学生储蓄银行；资助学生结社办刊；发起工读互助团，允许校外旁听生缴费注册听课，对偷听生也不防范；考试不再公布分数，甚至允许不要毕业文凭者可以不参加考试。在学校领导体制方面，按照教授治校的原则，成立由校长、各科学长和教授代表组成的校评议会，统领校政。决定学科废立，提出学校预算，制定和审核学校条令，审核教师学衔和学生成绩，一改校长独揽校政的传统。教授之辞退与聘任的最终决定权在教授评议会，非任何人可以独立辞退与聘任。教授在外兼职不仅只能拿讲师薪俸，而且没有选举教授评议员的权利。蔡元培还特意对教师资格作了规定："为官吏者，不得为本校专任教员。"各系建立教授会，选举产生教授会主任（系主任）、决定教务（如课程设置，选择教科书，考核学生成绩等）。由教授出任北大教务长、总务长，民主管理校务。蔡元培强调的是遵守法制前提下的民主，为此他侧重制度建设，认真修订了一系列大学管理规则，要求师生言行遵守校规。由蔡元培一手开创的新型大学运营模式至今仍然是难以逾越的时代巅峰。

各种社团纷纷成立，学校呈现一派生动活泼的局面。这是当时北京大学部分学生社团的章程。
Many societies were established and the fresh and vigorous fashion was in prevalent in University. These are some societies' regulations of Peking University at that time.

Beida's core principle of educational system reform is "academy foremost and governance by professors." Cai advocated the separation of academic school from technological school and the integration of arts and science. At the advice of Hu Shi, the "academic year" system was changed into credit system, and the elective system was adopted. The learning enthusiasm and initiative of students were mobilized for the convenience of individualized instruction. The determination of course selection was in the charge of postgraduates and preparatory professoriates respectively. For freshmen, freshmen advisory committee was specially established as the counselor of students in terms of their course selection. The elective system was first adopted in Beida in 1919, and was adopted by other universities in succession as of 1922. Beida founded academic research institute to promote academic independence; established consumption commune and students' saving bank; sponsored students to set up societies and run periodicals; initiated work-study mutual-aid society, allowed guest students outside Beida attend the class after payment and registration, it even turned a blind eye to eavesdroppers; if the students pass the exam, their scores would not be announced, and those who feel they don't need graduate diploma were permitted not to attend the final exam. In respect of leadership system of Beida, in line with governance of school by professors, a policy-making council made up of chancellor, deans of various divisions and representatives of professors was established to administer university affairs, decide the abolition and set-up of subjects, propose the budget of the school, work out and review school rules and regulations, and verify faculty's academic titles and scores of students. Therefore, the tradition of exclusive administrative power of chancellor had been changed thoroughly. The final decision regarding the dismiss and recruitment of professors was decided by the professor council, no one could dismiss or engage them independently; if a professor took a part-time job, he or she could only get the salaries as that of lecturers from Beida and had no right to be elected as a member professors of the council. Cai Yuanpei also made a rule for faculty members' qualification, "No individual could serve as a full-time professor while simultaneously holding government office." Various departments established professoriates and elected the directors of professororiates (deans) to make decisions on teaching matters (curriculum arrangement, selection of textbooks, check-up of students' performance, etc.). Professors were to act as the academic dean and dean of general affairs to carry out democratic administration of school affairs. The democracy stressed by Cai is on the premise of observance of laws, therefore, he laid emphasis on system construction, seriously modified a series of managing rules of school, and required the teaching faculty and students to observe the rules of the school. Even today, the novel university operation mode created by Cai Yuanpei is still a peak of time and insurmountable.

蔡元培刚到北大上任时，发现各学科开教务会议为照顾外籍教员，居然都要求用英语发言，他马上决定学校此后开会一律使用中文。有人提出疑义时，蔡元培反驳说，在自己国家的大学使用母语教学工作，理所当然，难道国外大学会为照顾中国籍教师而使用中文工作吗？

When he just took his post in Beida, Cai Yuanpei found that all members were required to speak English during faculty meetings of various departments in special consideration of foreign faculties. He immediately decided that Chinese was the only language used at all meetings of Beida afterwards. When someone questioned him about that, Cai Yuanpei snapped: it is natural to use your own language to teach in universities of your own country; would foreign universities speak Chinese for consideration of Chinese teachers?

顾颉刚在《蔡元培先生与五四运动》一文中记述："蔡元培为了贯彻自己的办学方针，还采取了一系列的有力措施。例如，在他的提倡下，学校成立了各种学会（最有名的有"少年中国学会"，由李大钊、邓中夏主持）、社团（如《新潮社》等）、研究会（如"马克思主义研究会"、"新闻研究会"、"书法研究会"、"画法研究会"等），还有"静坐会"等体育组织。学校还开音乐会，办体育运动会，允许成立学生自治会。校内思考和讨论之风盛行，无论在教师还是

学生中，都有左、中、右，有共产主义者、三民主义者、国家主义者、无政府主义者，有立宪派，甚至有帝制派、复古派（如中文系里的"国故派"）。从那以后，学生们打麻将、吃花酒的越来越少，研究学问和关心国家前途命运的越来越多。在蔡先生的主持下，北大名副其实地成了国内首屈一指的高等学府了。"

In his "Mr. Cai Yuanpei and May 4th Movement", Gu Jiegang relates, "In order to enforce his principle of running a university, Cai Yuanpei also took a series of effective measures. For example, under his suggestion, Beida founded various academies (the best known is "Youth China Association", presided by Li Dazhao and Deng Zhongxia), societies (New Trend Society, etc.), research societies (such as Marxism Research Association, News Research

1918年6月，王光祈、李大钊等人发起少年中国会。图为少年中国会部分成员合影。左起：二邓中夏、四张申府、八李大钊、九黄日葵（上图）
Wang Guangqi, Li Dazhao et al organized and founded Association of Young China in June 1918. A group photo of some members of Association of Young China. From the left, the second was Deng Zhongxia; the fourth was Zhang Shenfu; the eighth was Li Dazhao and the ninth was Huang Rikui. (the upper picture)

蔡元培发起成立北京大学画法研究会，以研究画法，发展美育为宗旨。图为华发研究会会员实习写生（中图）
Cai Yuanpei founded the Drawing Research Association whose aim was to research the techniques of drawing and develop aesthetic education. A member of Drawing Research Association was sketching.(the middle picture)

毛泽东、蔡和森等于1918年4月成立进步社团新民学会。五四运动后，将宗旨改为"改造中国和世界"。图为部分新民学会会员的合影（三排左八何叔衡，五排左四毛泽东）（下图）
Mao Zedong, Cai Hesen et al founded an advanced social groups-Xinming Society in April 1918. After the May 4th movement, its aim was changed into "To reform China and world". A group photo of some members of Xinming Society. (He Shuheng was in the third row, eighth from the left; Mao Zhedong was in the fifth row, fourth from left) (the lower picture)

Association, Calligraphy Society, Paintings Society), as well as sports organizations such as "sits-in society". Beida also held concerts, sports events, and allowed students to establish self-governing association. There was a prevailing atmosphere of thinking and discussion in Beida. No matter among faculty members or students, there were the left, in-betweens and right, communists, followers of the Three People's Principles, nationalists, anarchists, constitutionalists, even imperialists, traditionalists (e.g. purists of Chinese Studies Department). Ever since then, there were fewer and fewer students who played majhong or drunk, while more and more students became dedicated to researches and concerned about the nation's fate. Under the tenure of Cai, Beida became a real higher learning institution and is the best one in China. "

在招生制度方面，蔡元培提倡男女平等，从1920年春天开始招收女生入学，开创了我国大学教育男女生同校之先河。蔡元培提倡平民教育，从1917年暑假开始，改变招生中的重资格、看出身的旧办法，坚持通过考试和以考生考试成绩的优劣作为是否录取的标准，使许多有真才实学的平民子弟能够入学。 1918年4月14日，在蔡元培的积极倡议下，北大校役夜班正式开办。为全校工友办夜校，这是在北大历史上，也是在中国高等学校的历史上没有先例的创举。

In terms of enrolling system, Cai advocated equality between male and female. Since the spring of 1920,

1920年春天北京大学开始招收女生入学，图为北大三位女生
Peking University started to recruit girl students in 1920. These are three girl students of Peking University.

平民夜校
The Night School for Common Citizens

Bedia began to enroll female students, making it the first university in history where both male and female students were learning here. Cai called for civic education. From the summer vacation of 1917, he changed the old way of enrollment which emphasized qualification and family background and insisted enrollment based on exam and performance of students in the exam, thus opened door to commoners of real learning. On April 14, 1918, thanks to the active suggestion of Cai, evening classes were formally opened in Beida. To organize evening classes for all faculty members of Beida was an unprecedented epoch-making event in the history of Beida as well as in the history of higher learning institutions of China.

蔡元培不拘一格罗致人才，并借鉴西方大学的模式对北大进行大刀阔斧的改革，使北大发生了巨大的质的变化。诚如冯友兰所说："从1917年到1919年仅仅两年多时间，蔡先生把北大从一个官僚养成所变为名副其实的最高学府，把死气沉沉的北大变成一个生动活泼的战斗堡垒。流风所及，使中国出现了包括毛泽东同志在内的一代英才。"

Cai recruited competent people without limitation to one type or style and carried out drastic reform in reference to the mode of western universities, enabling great and essential changes to Beida. Indeed, as Feng Youlan remarked, "From 1917 to 1919, within only more than 2 years, Mr. Cai turned Beida from a bureaucratic place into an authentic higher learning institution, and turned the dull Beida into an active and vigorous battle fortress. This prevailing atmosphere gave rise

1918年1月15日在北京东城方巾巷15号华法教育会事务所举行华法教育会会议
Societe Franco-Chinoise d' Education meeting held by Societe Franco-Chinoise d' Education affair office at No.15 Fangjin Alley Dongcheng District Beijing on January 15, 1918

to the emergence of great talents like Mao Zedong in China."

蔡元培对于新文化运动的贡献便是提出了"思想自由、兼容并包"的文化包容论。1919年3月，文化保守派代表人物林纾曾发表致蔡元培的公开信，攻击新文化运动"覆孔孟，铲伦常"，"尽废古书，行用土语为文字"。蔡元培反驳说："对于学说，仿世界各大学通例，循'思想自由'原则，取兼容并包主义，与公所提出之'圆通广大'四字，颇不相背也。无论为何种学派，苟其言之成理，持之有故，尚不达自然淘汰之运命者，虽彼此相反，而悉听其自由发展。"蔡元培对林纾挑战的公开答复既是对旧派的沉重打击，又是对新派的极大鼓舞。

Cai's contribution to the New Culture Movement was that he proposed the theory of cultural tolerance the content of which was "freedom of thought and all-embracing openness to ideas". In March 1919, Lin Shu, a representative of cultural conservatives, ever published an open letter to Cai Yuanpei, attacking the New Culture Movement as "subvert Confucianism and Menciusism, eradicate ethics" and "denounce classics and apply plain language for writing". Cai retorted, "As to theories, we imitate the principle of "freedom of thought" commonly adopted in various universities around the world and adopt the theory of "all-embracing openness to ideas", which is not quite against the "flexibility and vastness" as you said. No matter what the school is, if its ideas sound reasonable and are based on reason while not to the extent of elimination by nature, though opposite to each other, they shall be entitled to pursue free development." The open reply of Cai to the challenge of Lin Shu was a heavy blow to the old

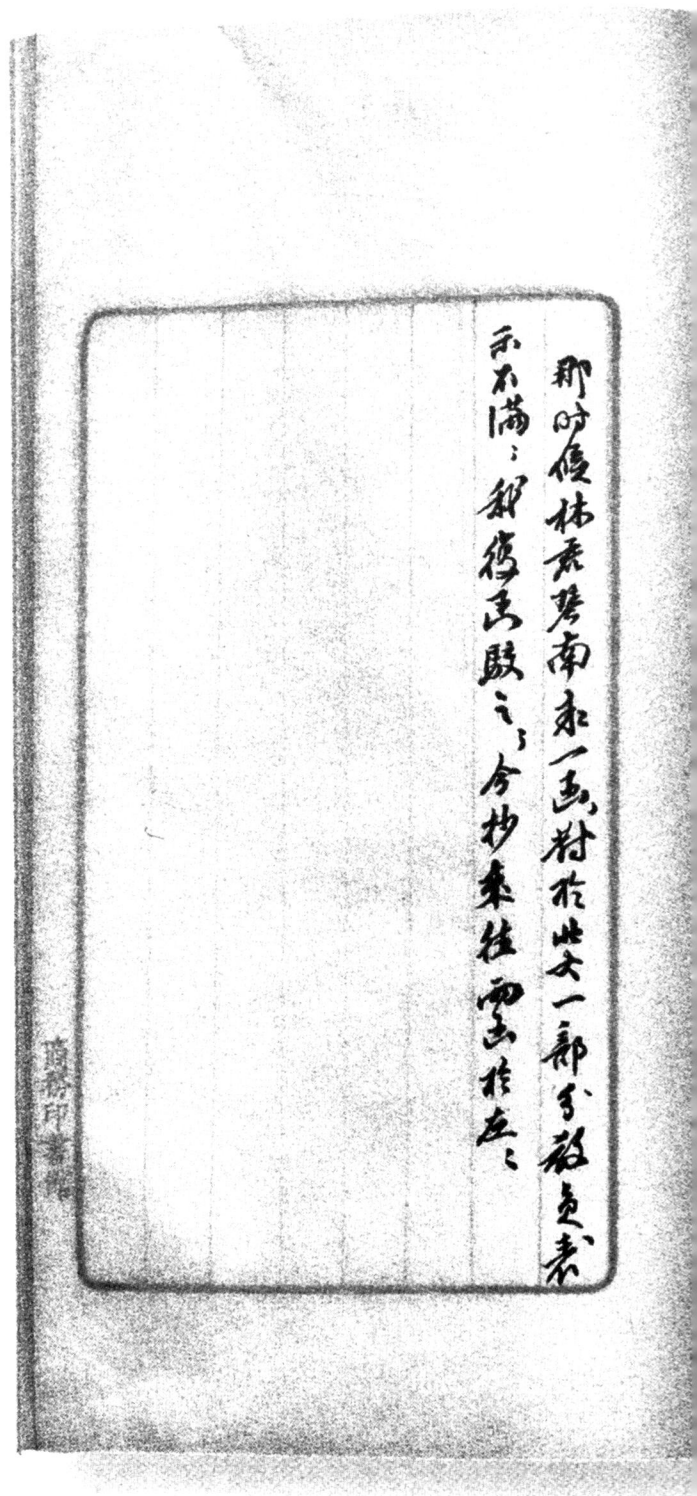

school as well as a great encouragement to the new school.

其实新文化运动的精神不在于提倡白话文、废除孔教，而是为近代中国请来两位先生：德先生（民主）和赛先生（科学）。不过，蔡元培认为科学是有局限的，并不能解决人生的所有问题。他说："治自然科学者，局守一门，而不肯稍涉哲学，而不知哲学即科学之归宿。"他指出："大学是包容各种学问的机关，我们固然要研究各种科学，但不能就此满足，所以研究融贯科学的哲学，但也不能就此满足，所以又研究根据科学而又超绝科学的玄学。"

As a matter of fact, the spirit of New Culture Movement didn't lie in advocating vernacular language and abolishing Confucianism, but in the two Sirs invited to China, they are Mr. Democracy and Mr. Science. However, Cai believed that science had its limitations and were incapable of solving all problems of human life. He said, "Those who study natural science, focusing solely on itself, was reluctant to be a bit involved in philosophy, unknowing philosophy is the destination of science." He pointed out, "Universities are institutions accommodating various studies. Though we need to study various sciences, we shall not be satisfied; we study the philosophy integrating and running through science, we shall not be satisfied either; therefore, we shall study metaphysics based on science but beyond science."

蔡元培认为大学是研究高深学问的机关，须实行"思想自由、兼容并包"的方针，才能促进学术的繁荣和发展。这一方针突出

蔡元培记述"兼容并包"思想的手稿
The manuscript with Cai Yuanpei's idea "all-embracing openess to ideas"

地体现在延聘教员方面。作为民主主义思想家，蔡元培首先聘请陈独秀、胡适、李大钊等新派人物担任北大教授。除此之外，他对确有真才实学的旧派人物，包括曾经拥护袁世凯复辟帝制的刘师培、顽固守旧的黄侃、反对共和的辜鸿铭以及尊孔为教的梁漱溟等人也予以聘任甚至破格聘任。蔡元培认为："大学者，'囊括大典，网罗众家'之学府也。《礼记·中庸》曰：'万物并育而不相害，道并行而不相悖'足以形容之。如人身然，官体之有左右也，呼吸之有出入也，骨肉之有刚柔也，若相反而实相成。各国大学，哲学之唯心论与唯物论，文学、美术之理想派与写实派，计学之干涉论与放任论，伦理学之动机论与功利论，宇宙论之乐天魂与厌世观，常樊然并峙于其中，此思想自由之通则，而大学之所以为大也。"这段文字生动具体地概括了蔡元培的大学观和学术观：思想自由，有容乃大。这是蔡元培教育思想的重要组成部分。正是在这样的大学观和学术观的指导下，北京大学出现了前所未有的学术自由、各派并存、百家争鸣的活跃局面。

In Cai's opinion, universities are institutions where profound knowledge is pursued and shall apply the principle of "freedom of thought and all-embracing openness to ideas", so that academic prosperity and development can be boosted. This principle was embodied outstandingly in recruiting faculty members. Cai, known as a democratic thinker, first recruited Chen Duxiu, Hu Shi, Li Dazhao and other new school figures as professors of Beida. In addition, he also recruited or broke the rule to recruit old school figures of real learning, such as Liu Shipei who ever supported Yuan Shikai to restore the monarchy, the stubborn and conservative Huang Kan, Gu Hongming who was against republicanism and Liang Shuming who respected Confucianism as a religion. To Cai, universities are learning institutions embracing great classics and various schools. "All things on earth grow together without one doing harm to another, all doctrines in the world develop in parallel with each other without coming into conflict" from *Middle of Road of Book of Rituals* is a sufficient explanation. Like human bodies, their

organs are in the left or right, people breathe in or out, and flesh and bone are soft and tough, which are opposite and complementary to each other. In various universities across the globe, immaterialism and materialism of philosophy, idealists and realists of literature and arts, the theory of interference and the theory of laissez faire in accounting, theory of motivation and utilitarian in ethics, the optimistic and pessimistic outlook of cosmology are often found in parallel. This is the common rule of freedom of thought and the reason of "greatness" of universities. The above text summarizes Cai's outlook on universities and learning in a vivid and concrete way: freedom of thought and all-embracing to ideas enable greatness. This is an important integral part of Cai's thought of education. It was right under the direction of such outlook on university and learning, Beida took on an unprecedented active scene characterized by academic freedom, coexistence of various schools and a hundred schools of thought contending with each other.

据资料记载，五四运动前后的北京大学，学术空气极其浓厚、热烈。各派专家学者或著文，或开设讲座，或登台授课，各抒

1917年1月26日，蔡元培、鲁迅出席京师图书馆开馆仪（左页上图）
Cai Yuanpei and Lu Xun were at the opening ceremony of Metropolitan Library in January 26, 1919. (the upper left picture)
1919年4月国语统一筹备委员会会员合影（左页下图）
The members of Preparatory Committee for Standardizing National Language in April 1919.
出席太平洋各国教育会议
Participating the education seminars of pacific nations (the lower left picture)

己见，各显神通。在北大三院礼堂里留美博士胡适正在用资产阶级观点讲授《中国哲学史》，与此同时在北大二院礼堂里则有旧学功底深厚的孔教派教员梁漱溟在讲孔孟之道。这二人的课都排在星期六下午，各讲各的观点、体系，让学生自由选择。在文字学方面，旧国粹派的黄侃和新白话派的钱玄同，观点针锋相对，互不相让，大唱对台戏。有一次钱玄同在讲课，对面教室里黄侃也在讲课。黄侃大骂钱玄同的观点如何如何荒谬，不合古训，而钱玄同则毫不在乎这些，你讲你的"之乎者也"，我讲我的"的了吗呢"。北京大学当时的情况颇为世人所称道。当时有人写文章说："我对北京大学的感情，近来极好．心目中总觉得这是现在中国唯一的曙光，其中容纳各派的学说和思想，空气新鲜得很。"

According to relevant materials, the academic atmosphere of Beida around "May 4th Movement" was extremely strong and fervent. Experts and scholars of different schools either wrote articles, or held seminars or lectured on the rostrum, speaking out their ideas and showing their special prowess. In the auditoria of No.3 yard of Beida, Hu Shi, a PhD who returned from USA, was lecturing *History of Chinese Philosophy* from the capitalist perspective, meanwhile Liang Shuming, a Confucian with a solid classical knowledge, was lecturing theories of Confucius and Mencius in the auditoria of No.2 yard of Beida. The classes of the two were both arranged in the afternoon of Saturday, they spoke out their own views and systems for the free choice of students. In respect of graphology, Huang Kan, an old purist, and Qian Xuantong, an upholder of vernacular language, had conflicting views and neither side would give way to the other, making a "tit for tat" scene. One time, Qian Xuantong was lecturing in class, so was Huang Kan in the opposite classroom. Huang Kan scolded Qian Xuantong for his ridiculous view incompatible with old traditions; while Qian Xuantong shrugged off this, "you lectured your old style while I lectured my new style". The situation of Beida then won great appraise from people. Someone wrote an article then, "My feeling for Beida has been wonderful these years. I always feel it is the only dawn light in China where various schools and thoughts coexisted, the air there is so much fresh."

当然，蔡元培主张"思想自由、兼容并包"也并不是没有原则，没有标准．没有界限的。从延聘教员来看，蔡元培是坚持很高的标准的，不光要有很高的学术水平，就是说要有强烈的学术追求，要站在世界科学的前沿，即便对国故也要用新方法来整理；还要热心教学，讲究教授法；另外还要为人师表，有好的道德修养，能成为"学生之模范人物"。正如当时北大学生所说，蔡先生请刘师培讲六朝文学但决不允许刘提倡帝制，请辜鸿铭讲英国文学但决不允许辜提倡复辟、反对共和。其次，兼容并包的各种学说必须"言之成理，持之有故，尚不达自然淘汰之运命"，否则是不会让其出现在北大讲堂上的。蔡元培对各派学说并不是一概包容，没有褒贬、扬抑的，相反是有所约束、

1918年，留法勤工俭学运动兴起。图为1919年3月15日，寰球中国学生会欢送第一批留法勤工俭学的学生启程。

The rise of The Movement of Going to France for Work and Study Program 1918. The Trans Global Student Union of China was seeing the first students off to France for work and study on March 15, 1919.

有所提倡的。作为一个民主主义革命家，他在各种场合对民主科学的新思潮、新学说、新观点给予了热情的支持和大力的提倡。正因为如此，北大才能成为新文化运动的中心、五四反帝爱国运动的发祥地、在中国传播马克思主义和民主科学思想的最初基地。蔡元培提出的"思想自由、兼容并包"的方针，在新旧思想激烈冲突、社会发生急剧变化的20世纪初叶，对于封建文化专制主义来说是一个具有革命意义的方针，是有利于新思想、新观点的存在、发展和传播的。也正是因为实行了这样的方针，民主科学思想乃至马克思主义才能出现在北京大学的学术舞台上，并以北大为基地迅速地传播开来。

Of course, Cai Yuanpei didn't upheld "freedom of thoughts and all-embracing openness to ideas" without any principle, criteria or limitation. Viewing from engaging faculty members, Cai adpted a very high standard. He required not only high academic level, that is, the faculty members should have fervent academic pursuit and stand at the frontier of world science; he even required new ways for traditional sinology, the faculty should also be enthusiastic about teaching and care about methodology; he also required teachers to be paragon of learning and virtue and models for students. Just as students of Beida then said, "Cai invited Liu Shipei to lecture the literature of the six dynasties, but forbade him to advocate monarchy, and asked Gu Hongming to teach English literature, but never allowed him to promote restoration or to voice against communism. In addition, various doctrines must be "sound reasonable, well-founded, not to the extent of elimination by nature", otherwise they would not be allowed to give lecture in classes". Cai didn't accept all doctrines without praise nor censure, on the contrary, he practiced some restriction and preference. As a democratic revolutionist, he gave vigorous support to and promoted greatly new trends, doctrines and views at various situations. It was just for this reason that Beida became the center of New Culture Movement, the origin of May 4th anti-imperialist patriotic movement, and the first base in China spreading Marxism and democratic and scientific thoughts. The principle of "freedom of thought and all-embracing openness to ideas" proposed by Cai was a principle of revolutionary significance to feudal cultural despotism in the early 20th century when new and old thoughts were in intense conflicts and society underwent drastic changes. It was favorable for the existence, development and dissemination of new thoughts and ideas. Thanks to the same principle, democratic and scientific thought, even Marxism, could appear on the academic stage of Beida and spread fast with Beida as the basis.

蔡元培的教育制度改革，为北京大学奠定了雄厚的人文自由精神基础。当年的北京大学实行政教分离，校长和教授不可以煽动学生从事政治活动。但是大学毕竟不是与世隔绝的象牙之塔，"往昔昏浊之世，必有一部分之清流，与敝俗奋斗，如东汉之党人，南宋之道学，明季之东林"。蔡元培认为大学要担负起"指导社会"的责任，培养学生爱国的公民道德。蔡元培解释说："为社会之一人，则以信义为本务，为国家之一民，则以爱国为本务。能恪守种种之本务，而无或畔焉，是为全德。"

Cai's reform of education system had laid a strong base of free humanity spirits for Beida. At that time, Beida adopted a separation between teaching and politics, and chancellor and professor were not allowed to instigate students to engage in political activities. But Beida was not an ivory tower isolated from the outside world, "In the past turmoil ages, there must be a clear stream fighting with bad social customs, such as party men of east Han dynasty, Confucian study of ethics of Southern Song dynasty and DongLin academicians of Ming Dynasty". In Cai Yuanpei's opinion, universities should shoulder the responsibility of "guiding the society" and cultivate students' patriotic sentiments. He further explained, "A person, as a part of the society, his essential duty is faith; to be a citizen of a country, his essential duty is patriotism. To be able to adhere to various essential duties without omission or violation is full morality."

五四运动中的学生领袖之一许德珩说：发动五四运动的主力是北京大学，而其精神上的指导者是蔡元培。陈独秀在《蔡子民先生逝世后感言》一文中说："五四运动，是中国现代社会发展之必然的产物，无论是功是罪，都不应该专归到那几

蔡元培在法国与华法教育会人士合影
The group picture of Cai Yuanpei and members of the China-France Education Society

个人。可是蔡先生、适之和我，乃是当时在思想言论上负主要责任的人。"周作人也称："蔡固系五四之首魁。"

Xu Deheng, one of the student leaders of the May 4th Movement said, "The major force that initiated the May 4th Movement was Beida, while the spiritual instructor was Cai Yuanpei." Chen Duxiu said in his "Feelings on the Death of Mr. Cai Jiemin" , "May 4th Movement is the inevitable result of social development of modern China, no matter it was credit or crime, it shall not specially attributed to those few persons. However, Mr. Cai, Shizhi and I were the main persons mainly responsible for the thoughts and speeches at that time". Zhou Zuoren also said, "Cai was definitely the forerunner of May 4th Movement."

五四首魁 赤子之心

Part3

Forerunner of May 4th Movement with a Patriotic Heart

1919年的中国，每一张日历上都满蓄着电光，一场自辛亥革命失败后渐蓄而成的新文化思潮，又因为历史的契机而成就了一场轰轰烈烈的爱国学生运动。1919年4月30日，巴黎和会对山东问题作出最后裁决，决定将德国在山东的一切权益均让给日本，并列入对德和约。正在巴黎以民间代表斡旋的梁启超得知这一消息，连忙致电当时的国民外交协会负责人汪大燮、林长民，建议警醒国民和政府，拒绝在和约上签字。林长民遂写成《外交警报敬告国人》一文，交由外交委员会事务员、北大预科讲师梁敬錞送至报馆，刊于5月2日的《晨报》头版头条。全文如下："胶州亡矣！山东亡矣！国不国矣！此噩耗前两日仆即闻之，今得梁任公电乃证实矣！闻前次四国会议时，本已决定德人在远东所得权益，交由五国交还我国，不知如何形势巨变。更闻日本力争之理由无他，但执一九一五年之二十一条条约，及一九一八年之胶济换文，及诸铁路草约为口实。呜呼！二十一条条约，出于胁逼；胶济换文，以该约确定为前提，不得径为应属日本之据。济顺、高徐条约，仅属草约，正式合同，并未成立，此皆国民所不能承认者也。国亡无日，愿合四万万民众誓死图之！"外交失败至此已经没有秘密可言。

In 1919, each page of the Chinese calendar was filled with lightning. Since the failure of 1911 Revolution, a new cultural trend gradually developed and evolved into a grand patriotic student movement because of historic opportunity. On April 30, 1919, Paris Peace Conference made the final decision on Shandong issue and decided to concede all privileges of Germany in Shandong to Japan and include this into Treaty of Versailles. After learning the news, Liang Qichao who was then in Paris mediating as a civil representative, sent a telegram immediately to Wang Daxie and Lin Changmin, principals of Council on Foreign Relation of National Government, advising and reminding citizens and government to refuse to sign on the treaty. Lin Changmin then wrote "Diplomatic Alarm to Chinese People" and entrusted it to Liang Jingchun, clerk of Council on Foreign Relations and preparatory lecturer of Beida, to send the article to newspaper office, the article was made a huge headline on the front page of *Morning Post* on May 2. The whole article runs as

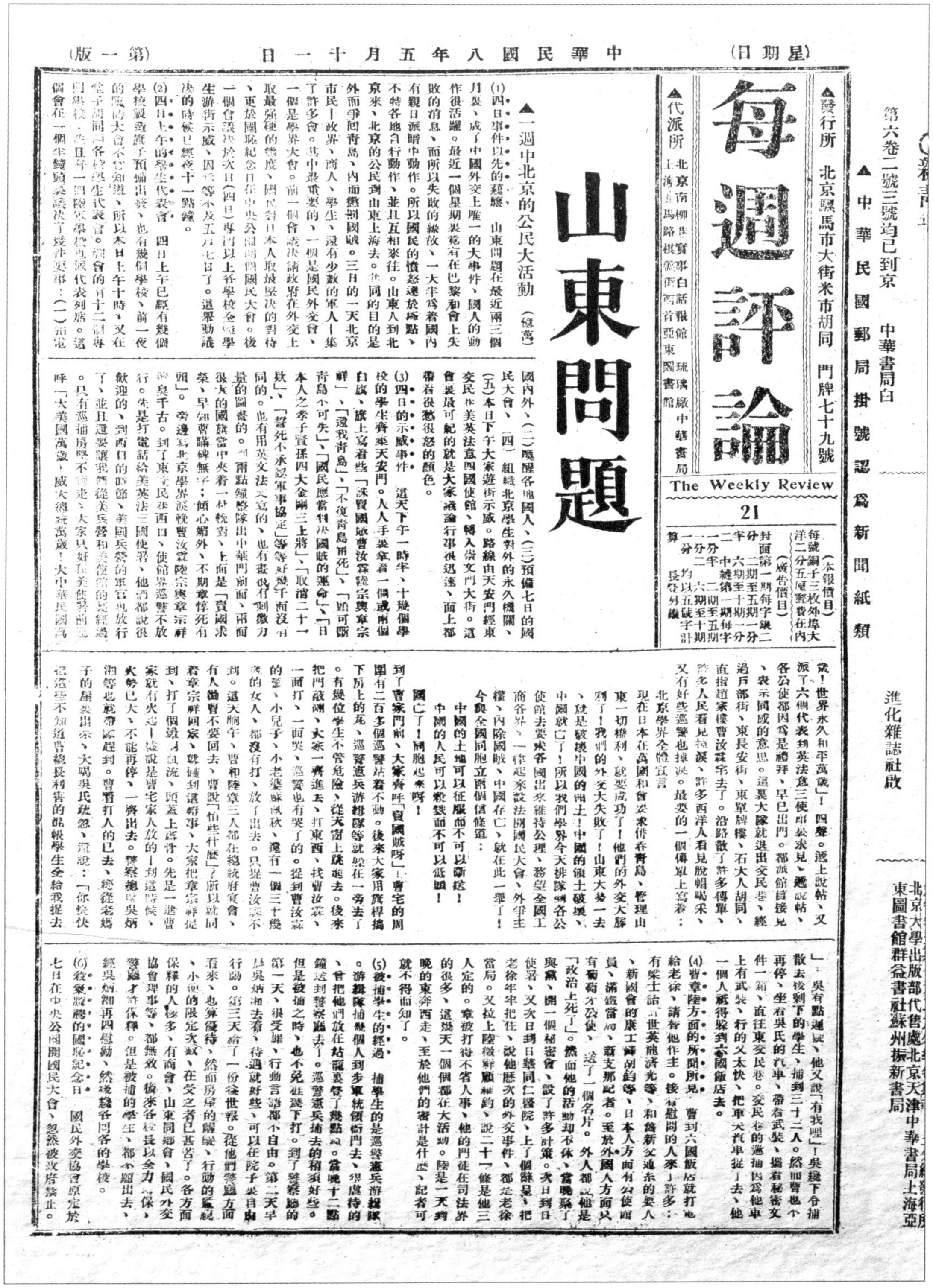

星期日　中華民國八年五月十一日　(第一版)

第六卷二號三號均已到京　中華書局白

▲中華民國郵局掛號認爲新聞紙類

進化雜誌社啟

北京大學出版部代售處　北京天津中華書局　上海亞東圖書館　群益書社　蘇州振新書局

每週評論

The Weekly Review

21

▲發行所　北京騾馬市大街米市胡同　門牌七十九號

▲代派所　北京南柳巷晨報館　琉璃廠中華書局　上海四馬路亞東圖書館

(本報價目)每號銅子三枚外埠大洋二分五厘郵費在內

(廣告價目)封面第一期至五期每字一分二，六期至十期每字一分，二十一期至五十期……，均以五號字計，長登另議

山東問題

▲一週中北京的公民大活動　(億萬)

(1)四日事件以先的醞釀　山東問題在最近兩三個月裏，成了中國外交上唯一的大事件，國人的動作很活躍。最近一個星期裏竟有在巴黎和會上失敗的消息，而所以失敗的緣故，一大半爲着國內有親日派暗中動作。所以國民的憤怒達於極點，不特各地自行動作，並且互相來往。山東人到北京來，北京的公民到山東上海去。共同的目的是外而爭回青島，內而懲罰國賊。三日的一天北京市民—政界、商人、學生，還有少數的軍人—集了許多會。其中最重要的，一個是國民外交會，一個是學界大會。前一個會議決請政府在外交上取最強硬的態度，國民對日本人取最堅決的對待，更於國恥紀念日在中央公園開國民大會。後一個會議決於次日(四日)專門以上各學校全體學生游街示威，因爲等不及五月七日了。這舉動議決的時候已經夜十一點鐘。

(2)四日上午的學生代表會　四日上午已經有幾個學校製造旗子預備出發，也有幾個學校，前一夜的臨時大會不曾知道，所以本日上午十時，又在堂子胡同法政專門學校開各校學生代表會。到會的有十二個專門學校，並且有一個陸軍學校也派代表列席。這個會在一個半鐘頭裏議決了幾件要事：(一)通電國內外，(二)喚醒各地國人，(三)預備七日的國民大會，(四)組織北京學生對外的永久機關，(五)本日下午大家遊街示威。路線由天安門經東交民巷美英法意四國使館，轉入崇文門大街。這會裏最可紀的就是大家議論行事很迅速，面上都帶着很懇很怒的顏色。

(3)四日的示威事件　這天下午一時半，十幾個學校的學生齊集天安門。人人手裏拿着一個或兩個白旗，旗上寫着些「誅賣國賊曹汝霖陸宗輿章宗祥」、「還我青島」、「不復青島寧死」、「頭可斷青島不可失」、「國民應當判決國賊的運命」、「日本人之孝子賢孫四大金剛三上將」、「取消二十一款」、「誓死不承認軍事協定」等等好幾千面沒有同的。也有用英文法文寫的，也有畫成有侮辱力量的圖畫的。兩點鐘整隊出中華門前面，兩面很大的國旗當中夾着一付輓對，上面是「賣國求榮，早知曹瞞碑無字；傾心媚外，不期章惇死有頭」。旁邊寫北京學界淚輓，曹汝霖陸宗輿章宗祥遺臭千古。到了東交民巷西口，使館界巡警不放行。先是打電話給美英法三國使署，他們都說很歡迎的，到西口的時節，美國兵營的軍官也放行了，並且還要讓我們從美兵營和美使館的裏經過。只有巡捕房堅不放走。大家只好在美使館前面高呼「大美國萬歲」、「威大總統萬歲」！「大中華民國萬歲！世界永久和平萬歲」！四聲。遞上說帖，又派了六個代表到英法意三使館要求見，遞說帖。各公使都因爲是禮拜，早已出門。都派館員接見，表示同感的意思。這裏大隊就退出交民巷，經過戶部街，東長安街，東單牌樓，石大人胡同，直指趙家樓曹汝霖宅去了。沿路散了許多傳單，許多人民看見掉淚，許多西洋人看見脫帽喝采，又有好些巡警也掉淚。最要的一個傳單上寫着：

北京學界全體宣言

現在日本在萬國和會要求併吞青島，管理山東一切權利，就要成功了！他們的外交大勝利了！我們的外交大失敗了！山東大勢一去，就是破壞中國的領土！中國的領土破壞，中國就亡了！所以我們學界今天排隊到各公使館去要求各國出來維持公理，務望全國工商各界，一律起來設法開國民大會，外爭主權，內除國賊，中國存亡，就在此一舉了！今與全國同胞立兩個信條道：

中國的土地可以征服而不可以斷送！

中國的人民可以殺戮而不可以低頭！

國亡了！同胞起來呀！

到了曹家門前，大家齊呼「賣國賊呀」！曹宅的周圍有二百多個巡警站着不動。後來大家用旗桿搗下房上的瓦，巡警憲兵游緝隊等就躲在一旁去了。有幾位學生不管危險，從天窗上跳進去。後來把門破開，大家一齊進去，打東西，找曹汝霖，一面打，一面哭，巡警也有哭了的。捉到曹汝霖的爹，小兒子，小老婆，蘇佩秋，還有一個三十幾歲的女人，都沒有打，放了出去。只是曹汝霖不到。這天晌午，曹和陸章三人都在總統府宴會，有人勸曹暫不要回去，曹說「怕些什麼」？所以就同着章宗祥回家，竟碰到這禍事，大家把章宗祥捉到，打了個半死，血流，頭蓋上露骨。先是一進曹家就有火起—據說是曹宅家人放的—到這時候，火勢已大，不能再停，一齊出去。警察總監吳炳湘等也就帶隊趕到。曹看打人的已去，總從老媽子的屋裏出來，大罵吳氏疏忽，還說：「你快快把這些不知道曹總長利害的混帳學生全給我捉去」。吳有點遲疑，他又說「有我哩」！吳幾下令捕散去後剩下的學生，捕到三十二人。然而曹也不再停，坐着吳氏的汽車，帶着武裝，揣着秘密文件一箱，直往東交民巷。交民巷的巡捕因爲他車上有武裝，行的又太快，把車夫汽車捉了去，他一個人祇得躲到六國飯店去。

(4)曹章陸方面的所聞所見　曹到六國飯店就打電給老徐，請着他作主。接着慰問的人來了許多：有梁士詒、王世英、施濟光等，和舊新交通系的要人、新國會的康士鐸胡鈞等，日本人方面有公使館員、滿鐵當局、新支那記者。至於外國人方面只有荷蘭公使，送了一個名片。外人都說他是「政治上死了」。然而他的活動卻不休，當晚就召集了與黨，開一個秘密會，設了許多計策。次日到日使署，又次日到日華同仁醫院，上了個辭呈，把老徐牢牢把住，說他歷次的外交事件，都是老徐當局。又拉上陸徵祥顧維鈞，說二十一條是他三人定的。章被打得不省人事，他的門徒在司法界的很多，這幾天一個個都在大活動。陸是一天到晚的東奔西走，至於他們的審計是什麼，記者可就不得而知了。

(5)被捕學生的經過　捕學生的是巡警憲兵游緝隊。游緝隊捕幾個人到步軍統領衙門去，很虐待的，曾把他們放在站籠裏督了幾點鐘。當晚十二點鐘送到警察廳去了。巡警憲兵捕去的稍須好些。但是被捕之時，也不免挨幾下打。到了警察廳的第一天，很受罪，行動言語都不自由。第二天早晨吳炳湘去看，待遇就好些，可以在院子裏自由行動。第三天給了一份益世報。從他們警廳方面看來，也算優待，然而房屋的齷齪，行動的監視，小便的限定次數，在受之者已甚苦了。各方面保釋的人很多，有商會，山東同鄉會，國民外交協會，理事等，都無效。後來各校長以全力保，警廳才許保釋。但是被捕的學生，都不願出去，經吳炳湘再四懇勸，然後纔各回各的學校。

(6)殺氣騰騰的國恥紀念日　國民外交協會原定於七日在中央公園開國民大會，忽然被政府禁止。

陈独秀、李大钊亲身投入爱国运动，他们创办的《每周评论》对五四运动具有重要的宣传鼓动和指导作用。这是《每周评论》出版的《山东问题》特号

Chen Duxiu and Li Dazhao devoted themselves into patriotic movement. They founded and published *Weekly Review* which played an important role in propagating, mobilizing and directing the May 4th Movement. This is the special issue of *Weekly Review* on the *Shandong Problem*

巴黎和会的外交失败，点燃了中国民众的怒火。1919年5月4日，北京学生3000多人聚集天安门前，举行游行示威，图为游行中的北大师生（左图）
The diplomatic failure in the Paris Peace Conference ignited Chinese people's rage. More than 3,000 students in Peking gathered in the front of Tiananmen Square for demonstration on May 4th, 1919. A photo of teachers and students of Peking University in demonstration (the left picture)
游行中的女生队伍（右图）
The teams of girl students in demonstration (the right picture)

follows, "Jiaozhou is lost, Shandong is lost, the nation is no longer a nation! The sad news reached me two days earlier, which was confirmed by the telegram of Mr. Liang and Ren! I heard that at the early four-nation conference, it was decided that the privileges of Germany in Shandong would firstly return to the five nations and then return back to our country, not knowing how much the situation has changed! I further heard that the excuses for Japan to covet the rights were no other than the Twenty-One Demands, Jiaozhou-Jinan exchange of notes, and protocols on various railways. Alas! The twenty-one demands was signed by coercion; Jiaozhou-Jinan exchange of notes was based on the demands and shall not be the proof that it belongs to Japan. Jishun and Gaoxu treaties are only protocols instead of formal contracts and are not concluded in fact, which are denied by all Chinese! The days of national subjugation can be counted with ten fingers! I wish our four hundred million compatriots will defend our nation with our lives!" There was nothing secret about the diplomatic failure then.

5月2日，蔡元培在北京大学饭厅召集学生代表和各班班长一百多人开会，讲述了巴黎和会牺牲中国主权的情况，指出这是国家存亡的关键时刻，号召大家奋起救国。当天在总统府，外交委员会已决议拒绝签约，汪大燮、林长民将致电代表团拒签电稿送呈徐世昌总统，徐阅后交给国务院准备拍发。不料国务总理钱能训却向正在巴黎参加和谈的中国代表团拍发密电，命令代表在合约上签字。国务院电报处一名职员连夜向林长民报告了消息，林长民当即向汪大燮汇报。外交委员会事务员叶景莘提醒说："北大学生亦在反对借款与签约，何不将消息通知蔡子民先生。"汪大燮即于5月3日凌晨专程前往东堂子胡同蔡元培家告知消息。

On May 2, Cai Yuanpei convened student delegates and monitors of various classes for a meeting at the Dining Hall of Beida and told them about China's sacrifice of territory at Paris Peace Conference, pointing out that it was the crucial moment of the survival of the nation and calling on all to save the country. In the presidential palace the same day, Council on Foreign Relations had adopted a resolution not to sign the treaty, Wang Daxie and Lin Changmin presented the telegram of no signing the treaty to President Xu Shichang, who handed it out to the State Council for cabling after reading it. Out of expectation, the Prime Minister Qian Nengxun sent a restricted message to the Chinese delegation then in Paris attending the negotiation and ordered them to sign the treaty. A clerk of the telegram office of the State Council reported that news to Lin Changmin that very night and Lin Changmin reported immediately to Wang Daxie. Ye Jingshen, a clerk of Council on Foreign Relations reminded,

五四演讲
A speech in the May 4th Movement

"Students of Beida also objected the loan and signature of the treaty, why don't we inform Mr. Cai Jiemin of this news?" In the early morning of May 3, Wang Daxie paid a special visit to Cai Yuanpei's residence at Dongtangzi alley to tell him the news.

胡适在1929年1月16日的日记中记述叶景莘所讲："巴黎和会中国代表团失败的消息传来，徐世昌主张签字，陆征祥、王正廷、伍朝枢皆主张签字。汪大燮其时为外交委员会主席，他于五月二日夜（三日夜）去看蔡元培，先以此时形势，说学生不可不有点表示。蔡赞成其说，故四日有大游行，遂有打赵家楼的故事。"叶景莘是汪大燮和林长民的重要助手，他在天津《大公报》发表《五四运动何以爆发于民八之五月四日》一文写道："外交委员会已开会决议，拒绝在巴黎和约上签字，报徐世昌核夺。但五月三日，林长民获悉：国务院已发出密电，令代表团签字。汪大燮焦急，叶景莘建议速告蔡校长。汪大燮即坐马车到东堂子胡同蔡子民先生家。当晚，蔡先生召集北大学生代表罗家伦、傅斯年、康白情、段锡朋等，告此消息。于是爆发五四运动。"梁敬錞后来也说："蔡校长亟召罗家伦、傅斯年、康白情、段锡朋，告以实况。""当时汪、林、蔡诸公之所为皆纯出于爱国与抗日之一念，绝无派系或个人情感杂于其间。"

In his dairy of January 16, 1929, Hu Shi recorded the words of Ye Jingshen, "When the news of failure of Chinese delegation at Paris Peace Conference spreads, Xu Shichang agreed to sign on the treaty, Lu Zhengxiang, Wang Zhengting and Wu Chaoshu all advocated to sign on the treaty. Wang Daxie was the chairman of Council on Foreign Relations, he paid a visit to Cai Yuanpei in the late evening of May 2 (May 3), saying that Chinese students should not sit still waiting for destruction in such an urgent situation. Cai agreed with his points, and here comes the big demonstration on the 4th and the story of attacking Zhaojialou." Ye Jingshen was an important assistant of Wang Daxie and Lin Changmin. He published an article "Why May 4th Movement Broke out on May 4th of the 8th Year of ROC" on *Takungpao Newspaper* of Tianjin, saying "the Council on Foreign Relations had adopted a resolution not to sign the Treaty of Paris and reported to Xu Shichang for decision; however, on May 3, Lin Changmin learned that the State Council had sent a secret telegram ordering the delegation to sign the treaty. Wang Daxie was anxious, Ye Jingyun advised him to inform chancellor Cai immediately. Shortly afterwards, Wang Daxie took a carriage to Mr. Cai Jiemin's residence at Dongtangzi Alley. The same night, Mr. Cai summoned student delegates of Beida Luo Jialun, Fu Sinian, Kang Baiqing, Duan Xipeng and others to inform them this news. Therefore, May 4th Movement broke out." Later, Liang Jingchun also said that chancellor Cai

五四爱国传单

The patriotic leaflet in the May 4th movement

called Luo Jialun, Fu Sinian, Kang Baiqing, Duan Xipeng together and told them the true situation. At that time, Mr. Wang, Lin and Cai were all acted out of the patriotism and anti-Japanese consideration, absolutely free of factions or personal emotions."

作为一位大学校长，一位教育家，蔡元培认为学生在学校应以求学为最大目的，不大赞成学生成立政治组织和参加政治运动。但是在具有划时代意义的五四运动中，在事关国家安危存亡的关键时期，他并不拘守这一观点，相反却以极大的同情与慈爱对学生的反帝爱国行动给予了坚决的支持和全力的保护。

As a university chancellor and an educator, Cai insisted that the pursuit of knowledge was the ultimate goal of students and was not quite in favor of establishment of political organizations or involvement in political campaigns. But during the epoch-making May 4th Movement and the crucial moment when the very life and safety of the country were endangered, he was not constrained by his original intention. On the contrary, he provided resolute support and all-out protection to the anti-imperialist patriotic activities of the students with utmost sympathy and compassion.

1919年6月1日，北洋政府取缔学生的一切爱国行动，出动军警镇压。图为军警逮捕学生。

The Northern Warlords Government banned all the students' patriotic activities, and dispatched the military police to quell. The Police were arresting students.

1919年5月7日，北洋政府迫于社会的压力释放五四游行当日被捕的学生，但对学生的各项要求置之不理。图为北京高等师范学校师生欢迎获释的校友。

On May 7, 1919, the Northern Warlords Government was compelled to release the arrested students, but ignored the students' requirements. The teachers and students of Peking Higher Normal College were welcoming the released students.

1919年5月4日下午，以北大为主力的各校学生3000多人到天安门举行集会和示威游行，随后愤怒的学生火烧了卖国贼曹汝霖的住宅赵家楼。军阀政府派军警抓走了32名学生，其中北大学生20人。当天晚上，蔡元培就邀请与司法部关系密切的王宠惠一起到北大法科大礼堂和同学们共同商议营救之事。他一再抚慰学生说："你们放心，被捕同学的安全，是我的事，一切由我负责。"夜里9时以后，他不顾劳累前去拜访曾帮助过他赴德国留学、现今受到段祺瑞敬重的孙宝琦，请求孙设法帮助解救被捕学生。孙宝琦表示为难，蔡元培则从晚9时到12时多一直呆坐在孙的会客室里。可以想见，为了解救学生，他当时的处境是多么尴尬和艰难。5月5日下午，14所学校的校长集中到北大开会，商讨如何营救被捕学生。蔡元培态度十分坚决地表示，为了保出学生，"愿以一人抵罪"。会上成立了以蔡元培为首的校长团，会后即到教育部、总统府、国务院疏通，但徐世昌等拒不接见。5月6日，蔡元培又率校长团先后到教育部、警察厅交涉，并以自己的身家性命作保，要求尽快释放学生。经过蔡元培等人的努力解救，加之社会舆论的压力，反动势力终于答应释放学生。5月7日，被捕学生获释，蔡元培亲自率领北大全体教职员和学生在沙滩广场列队迎接。大家见面分外激动，彼此相对欲言无语，许多人竟致大哭起来。蔡元培劝慰大家应当高兴，不要哭，话未说完自己也禁不住流下了眼泪。北大被捕获释学生许德珩在回忆当时情景时说："当我们出狱由同学伴同走进沙滩广场时，蔡先生是那样的沉毅而慈祥，他含着眼泪强作笑容，勉励我们、安慰我们，给我们留下了极为深刻的印象。"

In the afternoon of May 4, 1919, over 3,000 students from various universities with students of Beida as the major force assembled in front of Tian'anmen square and held a demonstration. Afterwards, the angry crowd burned down Zhaojialou, the residence of traitor Cao Rulin. Beiyang government sent military police and arrested 32 students, 20 of whom were Beida students. In the evening of the same day, Cai Yuanpei invited Wang Chonghui, who was in close relation with Ministry of Justice, to the auditorium of law department of Beida and discussed how to rescue the students arrested together in the presence of other students. Cai consoled the students again and again, saying "Please be assured, the safety of the arrested students is my concern and I will assume all responsibilities" After 9 o'clock in the night, despite his tiredness, he went to visit Sun Baoqi, who ever helped him to study in Germany and was then respected by Duan Qirui. Cai begged Sun Baoqi to help to rescue the arrested students. Sun expressed his difficluties, Cai then sat in his guestroom from 9 to past midnight of the next day. We can imagine that, in order to save the arrested students, what an embarrassing and difficult situation had Mr. Cai endured. In the afternoon of May 5, chancellors of 14 universities gathered together in Beida to deliberate how to rescue the students. Cai showed his strong resolution that he would like to be solely liable for this issue in order to get the students bailed out. At the meeting, chancellor team headed by Cai Yuanpei was founded and then they went to Ministry of Education, Presidential Palace and State Council for negotiation, but Xu Shichang and others refused to meet them. On May 6, Cai Yuanpei led the chancellor team to the Ministry of Education and Policy Agency again for negotiation, and required to release the students as soon as possible. To achieve this objective, Mr. Cai expressed that he would like to offer his life as well as all his properties as the surety. Through the efforts of Cai Yuanpei and others, in addition to the pressure of public opinion, the reactionary force finally agreed to release the students. On May 7, the arrested students were released and Cai Yuanpei led all faculty members and students to welcome them at Sandbeach Square. The students were excited to see each other. They had so many words to tell each other but not knowing to begin with what, at last many burst into tears. Cai Yuanpei persuaded them to be happy and not to cry, but his own tears rolled down without finishing his remarks. When recalling the scene then, Xu Deheng, one of the released Beida students, said, "When we were out of the prison and walked into Sandbeach Square accompanied by our schoolmates, Mr. Cai was so calm and kind. With tears in his eyes, he forced a smile, encouraged us and comforted us, which was deeply imprinted in my mind. "

在五四运动中，蔡元培虽然没有直接走到游行队伍中，但却起到了别人所替代不了的、爱国学生护卫者的巨大作用。为营救学生，保护学校，他不顾个人安危荣辱，日夜奔忙，费尽心力，不惜受慢待、坐冷板凳。当有人劝他"恐危

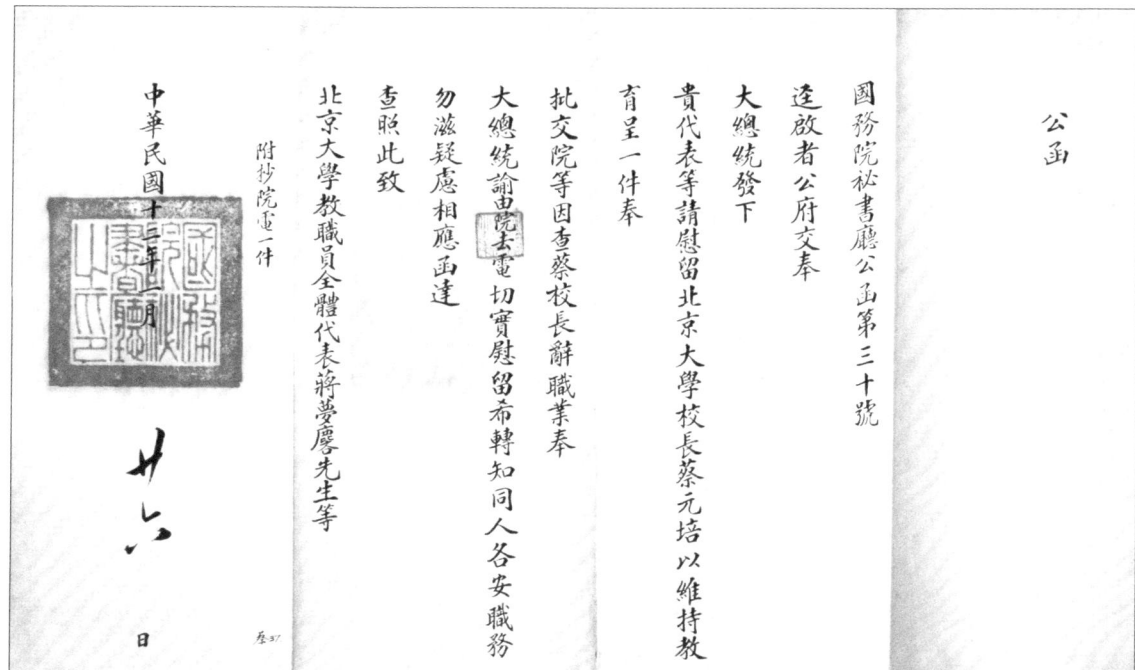

北大教职员工致函国务院秘书厅挽留蔡元培的公函
The official letter written by faculties and staffs of Peking University to the secretary office of state council for persuading Cai Yuanpei to stay

及君身"时，他笑着回答说："如危及身体，而保全大学，亦无所不可。"表现了他对祖国、对教育、对青年学生的深切热爱之情。

During the May 4th Movement, though Mr. Cai didn't join in the demonstration himself, he played an irreplaceable great role as an great protector of the patriotic students. In order to rescue the students and protect the school, without consideration of his own safety and honor, he busied day and night, exhausted his intellect, neglected others' insolence and cold faces. When someone reminded him he might be endangered, he answered with a smile: it is ok if my body is endangered while the school can be preserved, which shows his deep and earnest love for his own country, for education and for young students.

宽厚仁者 百世伟业

没有人怀疑蔡元培是中国现代史上最著名的教育部长、最成功的大学校长。他的成功似乎不在于他的学问和事功，而在于他的伟大人格。他那宽容、和蔼、慎独、淡泊、仁爱、谦让、真诚、民主、志趣、原则等优秀人格特色，像磁场一样吸引了当世最为著名的人才，与他一起，出一种风气，成就百世伟业。

Cai Yuanpei is undoubtedly the most renowned education minister and the most successful university chancellor in modern Chinese history. It seems that his success doesn't rest on his learning and achievements, but his great personality. His outstanding personalities such as tolerance, kindness, proper behavior even in private life, detachment, benevolence, humility, sincerity, democracy, ambitions and principles, which appealed to the most famous talents then like a magnetic field to cultivate a kind of ethos and make achievements enduring for centuries together with him.

大多数与蔡元培接触过的人，无不认为蔡是位和蔼可亲的人。尽管很多人摄于先生的大名，在未见面前总不免有些惶恐不安，但一交谈，就会使人很快精神放松，如浴春风。陈独秀曾说蔡元培哪怕是生气，"态度还很温和"。 冯友兰在《我所认识的蔡校长孑民先生》一文中，讲到他所亲历的两件事：一次，冯从新任的蔡校长身边走过，顿时"他的蔼然仁者、慈祥诚恳的气象，使我心里一阵舒服。我想这大概就是古人所说的春风化雨吧"。另一次，因事需要学校出一个证明书，按正常手续办来不及了。冯友兰大胆闯进校长室，直接去找蔡校长。蔡校长听完情况说明后，当场提笔写了几个字，并"亲切地交待"如何去文书科具体办理手续。这种不言之教，使冯友兰感受很深，几十年后都牢记在心，津津乐道，念念不忘。

Most people who had contact with Cai Yuanpei all believed that Cai was a kind and affable person. Awed by his fame, many felt unavoidably uneasy before meeting with him, but once they started conversation with him, they felt relaxed spiritually, as comfortable as bathing in mild breeze. Chen Duxiu ever said that Cai's attitude was mild even when angry. Feng Youlan related his two personal experiences in his "What I Know about Mr. Cai Jiemin", "Once I passed by Cai Yuanpei, this new chancellor, I was immediately struck by his benevolent, kind and sincere manner, which made me pleasant in heart. I guess this is the "life-giving spring breeze and rain" described by ancient people. Another time, I needed the school to issue a certificate for some matter, but it would be late if going through the normal procedures. I courageously burst into the Chancellor's Office to look for Chancellor Cai directly. After learning about the situation, Cai instantly wrote several words and explained amicably how to deal with specific procedures at the Documentation Division. Such wordless teaching was so impressive to Feng Youlan that he still remembered and take delight in talking about it after decades."

蔡元培和家人合影，前排左三为蔡元培
A photo of Cai Yuanpei and his families. Cai Yuanpei was in the front row, third from the left

蔡元培性情温和，日常无疾言厉色，无论遇达官贵人或引车卖浆之流，态度如一。这不是说蔡元培是个"好好先生"，没有阳刚之气。他对大是大非问题是严肃不苟的。北大曾发生"讲义费风波"。学生因不肯交讲义费，聚了几百人，要求免费，气势汹汹。蔡元培坚执校纪，不肯通融。一时秩序大乱。见此，蔡一改谦和温恭的形象，在红楼门口挥拳作势，怒目大声道："我跟你们决斗！"包围先生的学生们纷纷后退。这大概是蔡元培一生中唯一一次为了维护学校大局不得不发狠吧。

Cai Yuanpei was mild in disposition, never said harsh words or put on stern looks in daily life. He always adopted the same attitude towards everyone no matter they are dignitaries or vendors. This is not to say that Mr. Cai was

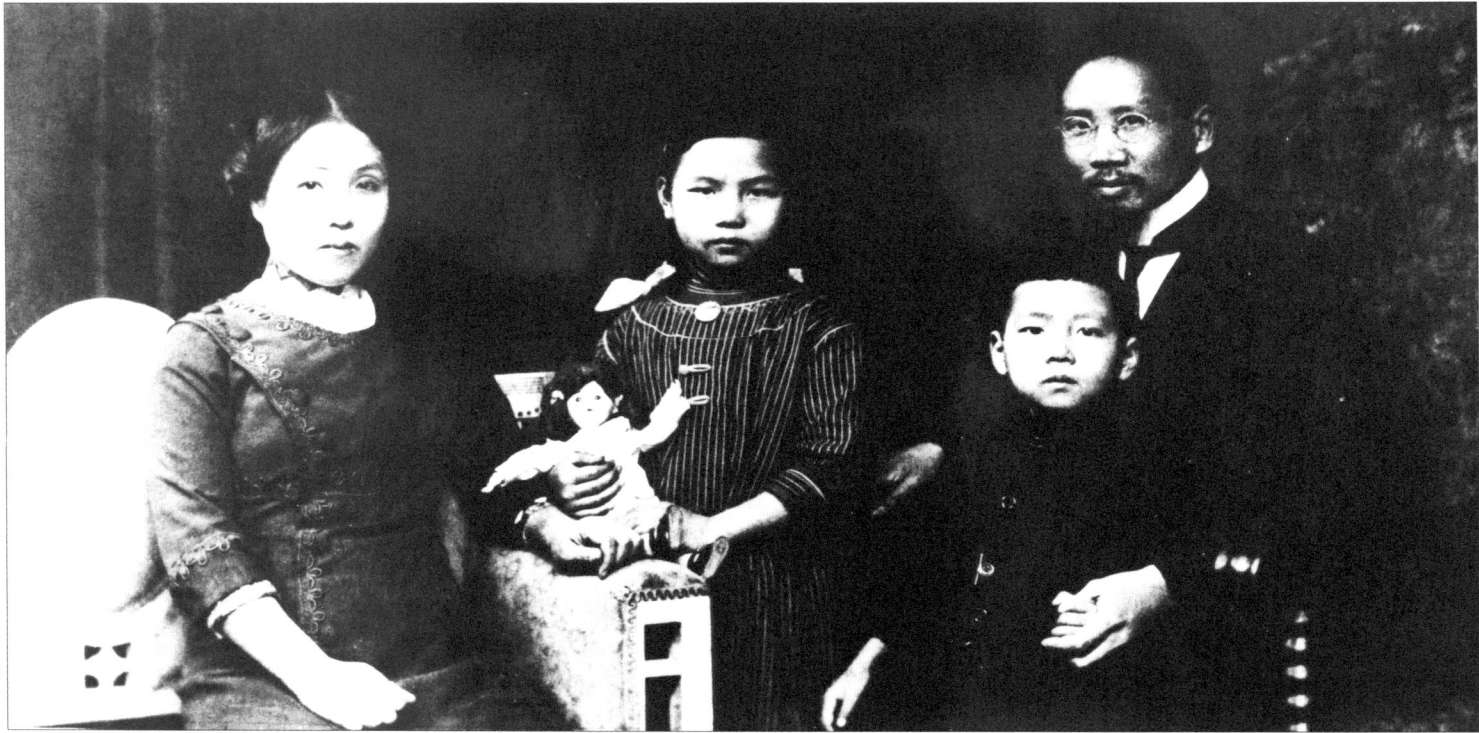

因不满袁世凯独裁，蔡元培辞去教育总长的职务，携夫人黄仲玉（左一）、女儿伯龄（左二）和儿子威廉赴欧洲游学。
Due to the dissatisfaction with dictatorship of Yuan Shikai, Cai Yuanpei resigned the job as Minister of Education and studied in Europe with his wife Huang Zhongyu (first from the left), daughter Bo ling (second from the left) and son William.

a Mr. Nice without masculinity. He was serious and rigid as to major issues of right and wrong. "Teaching materials fee event" ever took place in Beida. Several hundreds of students gathered as they refused to pay the teaching materials fee and demanded free supply of them, seeming quite truculent. Cai upheld the disciplines of school and would not bend the rules. At one time, a great disorder occurred. Seeing this, Cai discarded his humble and mild manner and waved his fist at the gate of the red building, and shouted with angry look "I fight duels with you!" The students around Mr. Cai retreated in profusion. This may be the only time that Mr. Cai had to be fierce in order to maintain the overall situation of Beida.

曾在爱国学社、民元教育部时期一直跟随蔡元培的老朋友蒋维乔，在《民国教育总长蔡元培》一文中写到"先生绝无耳目四肢之嗜好"，为爱惜生灵，而不愿杀生，持素食。蔡元培至德国后，亦曾听朋友李石曾谈到食肉的害处，正好他又看过俄国大文豪列夫·托尔斯泰著作中关于打猎惨状的描写，于是宣布不再食肉，还劝告朋友寿孝天说："蔬食有三义：一卫生，二戒杀，三节用。"并表明自己专食蔬食是因为戒杀。寿孝天回信引用杜亚泉的话说："植物未尝无生命，戒杀义不能成立。"对此，蔡元培说："戒杀者，非伦理学问题，而是感情问题。"他解释说，蔬食者不是绝对不杀动物，一叶一水中也不知道有多少动物，但因为常人无法看见，所以感情也未能顾及。而对于能够看见的动物，感情则可以顾及，所以要戒杀。蔡元培坚持素食12年，直到1921年10月因患糖尿病、左下腿溃烂住进德国医院治疗，医生认为由营养不全面引起，经劝告后又肉食。

Jiang Weiqiao, an old friend of Mr. Cai Yuanpei who had been following Mr. Cai during the period of Patriotic Study Society and Ministry of Education of 1911 Revolution, said in "Education Minister Cai Yuanpei of Republic of China", "Mr. Cai was in no way addicted to any animal body, he had been a

1923年7月，蔡元培与第三任夫人周骏女士在苏州留园结婚。
Cai Yuanpei and his third wife, Zhou Jun, got married in Liuyuan Garden, Suzhou in July 1923.

vegetarian in order to cherish and protect lives. After arriving in Germany, he also heard his friend Li Shi telling about the harms of eating meat. It happened that he was reading a work written by Russian literary giant Leo Tolstoy describing the miserable scene of hunting, so Mr. Cai proclaimed that he will never eat meat any more. He also persuaded his friend Shou Xiaotian by saying that vegetables had three advantages: sanitary, no killing, and economic, and made clear that he ate only vegetables for no killing. Shou Xiaotian replied by quoting the words of Du Yaquan, 'plants might not be lifeless, so the significance of no killing can not hold true'. With this regard, Cai Yuanpei said, 'No killing is not a matter of ethnics, but a matter of feelings.' He explained that it was not that vegetarians were not to kill animals absolutely, no one knew how many creatures were there even in a leaf or a drop of water, but as common people could not see, so they could not concern about them emotionally. As for visible animals, we could attend to them emotionally, so we should not kill." Cai Yuanpei had been a vegetarian for 12 years until he was hospitalized for diabetes and canker of his lower left leg. The doctor believed his illness was caused by malnutrition and he was then persuaded to have meat again.

作为北大校长的蔡元培，每月收入有600块大洋，在当时也算是不错的了，但是他依旧生活简朴，平时三餐也很简单，他的夫人说他："稀饭也吃，干饭也吃，焦饭也吃。"在北大任校长期间，他的午餐同教师一样。段锡朋回忆说："有一次走过校长室门前，一个小饭铺伙计提着菜篮，说是送饭给校长吃，我就打开盖子看一看，一碟木樨炒肉，一碟醋溜白菜和几个馒头。我们当穷学生的总以为校长每饭所用，虽不是山珍海味，总亦离不了三盘四碗，谁知道竟是这样。其实他老先生一生都是这样。"

As the chancellor of Beida, Cai Yuanpei's monthly income was 600 silver dollars, which was quite a lot then. But he still led a simple life, even his three meals were very simple. His wife said, "Rice juice is ok for him, so are cooked rice and even burnt rice." When he served as chancellor of Beida, his lunch was the same as that of teachers. As recalled by Duan Xipeng, "One time, I passed by the door of the chancellor office, an errand boy of a small restaurant carried a basket and said he was delivering food to the chancellor. I opened the lid and saw a dish of stir-fried pork shreds and cabbage with fungus and scrambled eggs, a dish of cabbage with sweet and sour sauce, and some buns. As a poor student then, I always thought it was natural that each meal of the chancellor, though not delicacies, had several dishes, it turned out to be that unexpectedly! In fact, he lived his whole life in that way."

蔡元培唯一的嗜好就是喜喝绍兴黄酒，年轻时是有名的"酒量如海"，爱劝酒，通常就餐常常只喝酒不吃饭。每年他都托亲友从绍兴买上数坛黄酒运去，备在家中自饮或请客。下酒菜也大多是绍兴特产，如干菜、霉干张等。逢年过节，他还要托亲友给他邮寄酱鸭、糟鸡、鱼干等绍兴年货。就连他平时用的酒壶也是从绍兴带去的锡制酒壶，里圆外方，中有夹层，天冷时可充灌热水温酒。一些好友说他"每饭必酒"，但他很有节制，平时自斟自饮，每餐以旧时四两为度。但偶遇知交旧好，相与宴饮，有时亦不惜一醉。后因胃病复发，每次限酒一小盅。

His only love was Shaoxing rice wine and he was famous sponge when young. He liked persuading others to drink, often drank only wine during meals. Every year, he would ask his relatives or friends to buy several jars of rice wine and bring them to his home for his own enjoyment or for treating guests. The accompaniments to drink were mostly specialities of Shaoxing, such as dry vegetable, fermented thousand layers, etc. On New Year's Day or other festivals, he would also ask his relatives or friends to post him Shaoxing goods for the Spring Festival like sauce duck, cold chicken cooked in wine, dried fish and others. Even the flagon he used usually was a tin one brought from Shaoxing. It was square outside and round inside, with an interlayer. Hot water could be poured into the interlayer to warm the wine when it was cold. Some friends said that he had wine every meal, but he was a moderate drinker. When he drank alone, the limit for him was 4 taels of wine each meal. However, when meeting old friends and drinking together, he would like to drink to his heart's content. Later, he was limited to have one small cup of wine each time due to the reoccurrence of his stomach disease.

1917年3月，蔡元培加入中国科学社，以北大校长的身份每月支助中国科学社200元。图为中国科学社社友合影。（前排右一蔡元培）
Cai Yuanpei as chancellor of Peking University assisted the Science Society of China with 200 Yuan every month. A group photo of the members of the Science Society of China. (Cai Yuanpei was in the front row, first from the right)

作为北大校长的蔡元培日理事项繁多，有时连吃饭的时间也不得闲。一天中午，蔡元培在北大校园一个亭子里吃饭，这时一群人拥着两个相互拉扯的学生来找校长，学生甲说学生乙打了他，要校长评理。蔡元培不紧不慢，对甲说："如果你不该打，他打你，他是妄人，你不必和妄人计较；如果你该打，他打你，你自己看着办吧。"两学生听了此话，不发一言，躬身退出，众人也都随着散了。

As the chancellor of Beida, Cai had a multitude of things to deal with every day and sometimes was not idle even during meals. One noon, Cai was dining in a pavilion of Beida. At that time, a group of people crowded round two students tangled up to see the chancellor. Student A said that student B beat him and asked the chancellor for reasoning. Cai said unhurriedly to A: if you should not be beaten while he beat you, he was an ignorant and rash person, you didn't need to be angry with an ignorant person; if you deserved the beat and he beat you, you judge it yourself." At his words, the two students said nothing and retreated with bows. The crowd also dispersed.

蔡元培有早起晨练的习惯。据他回忆，小时经常熬夜苦读，"有一次，母亲觉得夜太深了，人太倦了，思路不能开展了，叫我索性睡了。第二天黎明叫起，此时竟一挥而就。从此，终身觉得熬夜不如起早，是被母亲养成的。"蔡元培认为："有健全之身体，始有健全之精神；若身体柔弱，则思想精神何由发达？ 或曰，非困苦其身体，则精神不能自由。然所谓困苦者，乃锻炼之谓，非使之柔弱以自苦也。"蔡元培推崇武术，曾对武学泰斗孙禄堂执弟子礼。他还说过："外国的柔软体操可废，而拳术决不可废。""中国的太极拳是有百利而无一害的国粹。"在他的支持下北大成立了"技击会"，师生中参加者甚多。蔡元培大力支持蒋维乔在北大开设讲坛教授"因是子静坐法"，并购买了几百个蒲团，免费供给愿学静坐的师生使用。

Cai had a habit of doing morning exercise. According to his memory, he was always toiling at his studies at night. "once my mother thought it was too late and I was too tried, so my thought was constrained, she then asked me to sleep. In the next morning when I woke up, I soon finished it with a single heat. From then on, I believed in all my life that getting up earlier was better than staying late at night, this habit was formed thanks to my mother. " In Cai's opinion, "Only the physical body is sound, can the spirit be wholesome; if the body is weak, how can the brain be developed? The spirit can not be free if the body is not tribulated. The so-called "tribulation" is exercise, other than sufferings weakening oneself." Cai Yuanpei spoke highly of martial arts and ever honored Sun Lutang, a martial arts guru, as his teacher. He also said, "The flexible gymnastics of foreign countries can be abolished, but never Chinese boxing", "Tai Chi is a national essence with every advantage, and no disadvantage" Under his support, Beida established Technical Boxing Society, in which a lot of teachers and students participated. He provided vigorous support to Jiang Weiqiao to lecture Master Yanshi's Meditation Method in Beida, and purchased several hundreds of cushions for the free use by the faculty and students for meditation.

蔡元培一生对坐轿最为反感，他认为用人抬人是不人道的，而且两人甚至三四人为一个人代步也不经济。人力车夫一个人拉一个人，经济倒是经济，但眼睁睁看到人家伛偻喘气出汗，实在大为不忍。他认为脚踏车和摩托车最为文明，不得已时坐马车。实在没有办法要坐人力车时，他首先问好价钱，一到即付钱，绝不还价。蔡元培就任北大校长，很长一段时间都是步行上班的。一次，蔡元培拜访孙宝琦，孙送客时见门前无车辆，就对蔡元培说："你现在不可以再徒行了。"蔡点头说是。第二次来时又是如此，孙便将自己的马车送给他。过了一些时间因事来访，孙未见所赠马车，等蔡走后，便派人将自己常用的一匹马送去。后来，蔡元培就每天坐这辆马车上午九点准时到北大第一院上班。据说当年北大教授们都只坐人力车，只有马寅初乘用中国银行的马车。坐马车是校长应有的体面。

Cai showed his utmost antipathy against taking sedan chairs, holding it as inhuman to use men to carry men and it was also not economic to use two or even three or four to walk for only one person; one rickshaw wallahs carried one person, it was economic indeed, but it was really unbearable to see others bending their bodies, gasping and sweating. He considered bicycle and motorcycle the most civilized, horse-drawn carriage could be taken at a push. If he had to take a rickshaw, he would first make sure about the price and make the payment immediately upon arrival and would never bargain. When he was the chancellor of Beida, he walked to work and kept this habit for quite a long time. One time, Cai Yuanpei visited Sun Baoqi. When seeing Cai off at the door, Sun found no vehicle in front of his door and then said to Cai, "You shall not walk again this time." Cai agreed with a nod. It turned out to be the same when he made the second visit, Sun then offered his own carriage to him. After some time, Cai called on again for some matter, Sun didn't see the carriage he offered. After Cai left, he order someone to send a horse frequently rid by him over to Cai. Later on, Cai took this carriage to arrive at No. 1 yard of Beida on time at 9 AM. It is said that professors of Beida all took rickshaws, only Ma Yinchu took the carriage of Bank of China. Taking carriage should be the decency deserved by chancellors.

帮助青年学生解决学业、生活方面的困境，蔡元培总是不遗余力。胡适在北大创办了"成美学会"，目的是效古君子成人之美，由教授们捐钱资助热心向学却家境贫寒的学生。蔡元培是最主要的赞助人之一，不仅个人捐款100块大洋，还鉴于个人力量的有限而将之划归学校统一办理，责成由胡适等四教授修订该会章程。北大有困难的学生若得到审核同意，可以借钱以应需要。如家境困难的学生陈顾远就通过蔡元培联系成美学会借到急需的100块大洋。

Cai Yuanpei always spared no effort in helping young students about learning difficulties and life problems. Hu Shi established "Help Accomplish Goal Society" in Beida in order to follow the example of ancient noblemen to help others to accomplish their goals. Professors would donate money to sponsor diligent but poor students. Cai Yuanpei was one of the most important sponsors. He not only donated 100 silver dollars, but also placed the society under the unified management of the school in consideration of limited personal strength and instructed Hu Shi and other three professors to revise its Constitution. Students of Beida in difficulty could borrow money to meet their needs if approved by examination and review. For example, Chen Guyuan, a student of Beida from a poor family, borrowed the critical 100 silver dollors by contacting the Help Accomplish Goal Society through Cai Yuanpei.

蔡元培经常为他人作保。有一位考取北京大学的新生叫马元材，得知要交一份由在京做官的人签名盖章的保证书，才能予以注册，便给蔡元培校长写信道："我不远千里而来，原是为了呼吸民主空气，养成独立自尊的精神。不料还未入学，就强迫我到臭不可闻的官僚面前去磕头求情，未免令我大失所望。我坚决表示，如果一定要交保证书，我就坚决退学。"几天后居然收到蔡元培校长的亲笔回信："弟元材谨启"，只见信中写道："查德国各大学，本无保

1940年3月11日，香港各界万余人公祭蔡元培先生
Over ten thousand people from all walks of life in Hong Kong mourning Mr. Cai Yuanpei on March 11, 1940

1940年3月5日，蔡元培在香港病逝。图为蔡元培灵柩送至香港东华义庄时，有北大同学扶柩下车。
On March 5, 1940, Cai Yuanpei died of illness in Hong Kong. When sending Cai Yuanpei's coffin to Tung Wah Coffin Home, students from Peking University were moving the coffin off.

证书制度，但因本校是教授治校，要改变制度，必须由教授会议讨论通过。在未决定前，如先生认为我个人可以作保的话，就请到校长办公室找徐宝璜秘书长代为签字盖章。"

Cai Yuanpei often act as guarantor of others. There was a freshman enrolled into Beida named Ma Yuancai. After learning that he could go through the registration only after handing in a guarantee signed and stamped by an official in Beijing, he then wrote to Chancellor Cai, saying "I came here despite the long distance and my original intention was to breathe the democratic air and develop an independent and self-respect spirit. Out of my expectation, before I enter the university, I am forced to beg the stink bureaucrats, which rather let me down. I have made a firm decision that if I am definitely required to turn in a guarantee, I will resolutely quit Beida." Several days later, he received a reply from

Chancellor Cai in person, with "To Brother Yuancai" written on the cover. The letter reads "I have checked various universities of Germany and there was no system of guarantee at first. As Beida adopts governance by professors, a resolution must be adopted through discussion at the professoriate in order to change the system. Prior to any decision, if you believe that I can be a guarantor myself, please come to my office to find secretary-general Xu Baohuang for signature and stamp on my behalf."

青年毛泽东在长沙求学时曾精读过蔡元培翻译的《伦理学原理》，在书的空白处竟写了150多条共计12000字的批注。1918年8月19日，毛泽东、萧瑜等湖南新民学会会员为赴法勤工俭学来到北京。因路费所剩无几、外语又不过关，毛泽东决计留在北京实行工读计划。虽然一个月的生活费只要五六块钱，可是毛泽东也无法筹到这笔款子，他必须寻找一个维持生活的职业。于是，萧瑜和蔡和森等人写信给蔡元培校长，"要求他雇用我们的一个无法赴法国的同伴为校内的清洁工人。蔡元培先生是位了不起的人，他看了我们的信后，立即就明白这是怎么一回事。但他有更好的主意，没有让他去做清洁工人，而是到校内的图书馆去工作。因此他写了一封信给北大图书馆馆长李大钊先生，信中说：毛泽东需要在本校求职，使其得以半工半读，请在图书馆内为他安排一职。"据北京大学档案中所存的工资发放册记载，毛泽东签收过三个整月的工资，月薪为8元。1919年10月毛泽东取得由北大新闻学研究会会长蔡元培签发的半年听讲证书。1920年1月，杨开慧的父亲杨昌济教授去世时没有给遗属留下赡养费，蔡元培发起募捐，征集赙金并率先捐款。该款后来被杨家用于资助毛泽东在长沙经营文化书社。1922年蔡元培因"全与我的理想相合"，十分欢喜地为毛泽东创办的湖南自修大学题词。

When studying in Changsha, young Mao Zedong ever read intensively *Principia Ethica* translated by Cai Yuanpei and wrote as many as 150 annotations totaling 12,000 characters at the blank space. On August 19, 1918, Mao Zedong, Xiaoyu and other members of Hunan New Citizen Society came to Beijing for the program of work-study in France. As limited travel expense was left and his foreign language was below the criteria, Mao Zedong decided to stay in Beijing to implement his work-study plan. Though life expenses each month cost were only 5 or 6 silver dollars, Mao could not raise the money and must find a life-sustaining job. Then, Xiao Yu and Cai Hesen wrote to Chancellor Cai and required him to employ a companion who could not go to France to be a cleaner of Beida. Mr. Cai was a great person and immediately understood the matter after reading our letter. But he had better solution. He didn't let Mao to be a cleaner but to work in the library. Therefore, he wrote a letter to Mr. Li Dazhao, the librarian of Beida, saying: Mao Zedong need a job in Beida to enable his study-work plan, please find a position for him in the library." According to the payroll saved in the archives of Beida, Mao Zedong signed for salaries of three complete months and his monthly salary was 8 silver dollars. In October 1919, Mao Zedong received a half-year certificate of class attendance issued by Cai Yuanpei, chairman of Peking University Institute of Journalism. In January 1920, when Professor Yang Changji, the father of Yang Kaihui, passed away, he didn't leave any maintenance, Cai Yuanpei solicited contributions, collected money for her family and took a lead in donation. The money was later used by Yang's family to sponsor Mao Zedong to run Culture Press in Changsha. In 1922, for "all agreeing with my ideal", Cai Yuanpei gladly inscribed a message for Hunan Self-study University founded by Mao Zedong.

蔡元培资助过一位幼年丧父的马姓远房表亲在北京生活、学习，直到他顺利地从北大俄语系毕业。许德珩回忆说："我因家里穷，蔡先生帮助我找了个翻译工作，每月挣十元钱，维持学费。"后来许德珩能够留学法国，也是依靠蔡元培多方筹资方能成行。甚而连回国后的工作也亏得蔡元培介绍。蔡元培还帮助北大画法研究会导师徐悲鸿赴法国留学。

Cai Yuanpei ever sponsored a distant cousin surnamed Ma whose father died early to live and study in Beijing until he smoothly graduated from Department of Russian of Beida. Xu Deheng recalled, "Since my family was

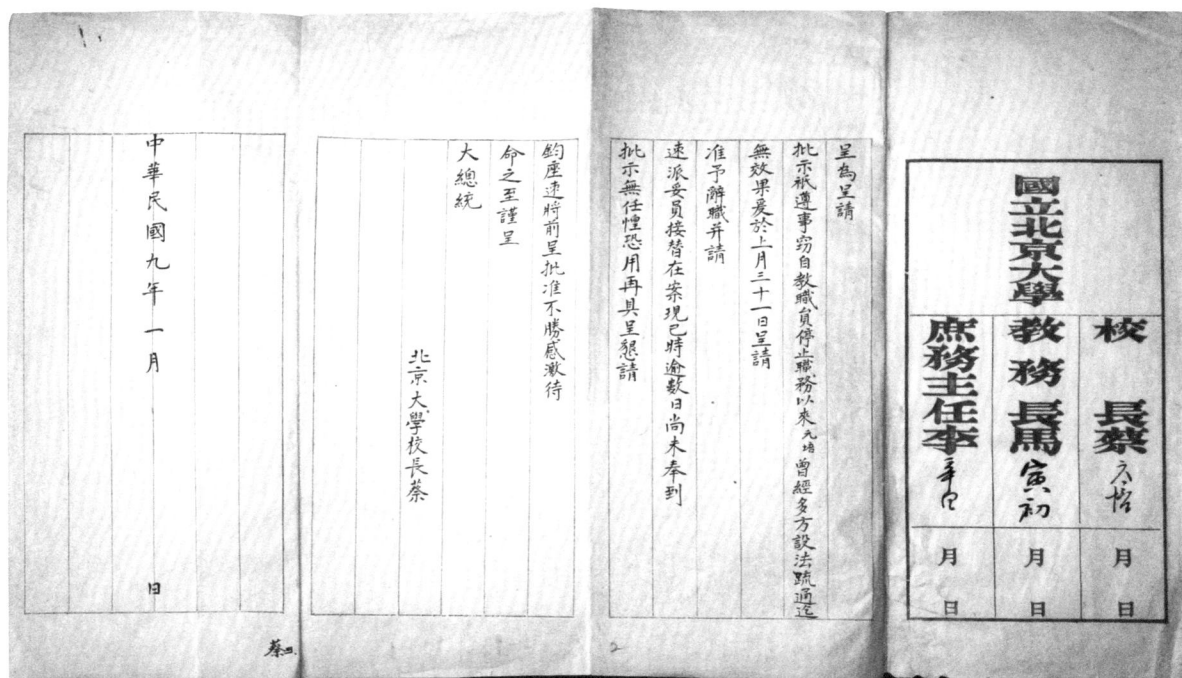

poor, Mr. Cai found me a translation job and I could earn 10 silver dollars each month to support my study."
Xu's study in France later was also enabled by Cai Yuanpei who raised money from various sources. Even his job after returning China was introduced by Cai Yuanpei. Cai Yuanpei also helped Xu Beihong, instructor of Painting Research Society of Beida, to go to study in France.

蔡元培多次带头发起捐资建校活动，并具名领衔发起工读互助团的《募款启事》。蔡元培曾阐明平等的精义："人人应该以服务为目的，而不以夺取为目的。"蔡元培勤于见客，勤于荐人，乐为周济扶助。他只要有闲暇，无论在早餐以前或迟至深夜，有客来总是接见的。凡是谁作一本书，求他作序或题签，他没有不答应的。求他八行书荐事，他也拿起笔来给你推荐。蔡元培因应酬较多，对社会公益组织和北大师生频繁捐助，每月薪资几乎不敷开支。甚而有时须靠夫人黄仲玉卖画补贴家用。

Cai Yuanpei run ahead many times to initiate donations for building the school and signed his own name to launch the *Notice of Donation Solicitation* of Study-work Mutual Aid Society. Cai ever explained the essence of equality: the aim of everyone shall be service, other than seizure. Cai often met with guests and recommend others, and was glad to provide assistance and support. As long as he had the time, no matter before breakfast or late in night, he would always open his door to visiting guests. He never refused to write a preface or inscription for a new book completed by anyone. If someone asked him to write a recommendation letter, he would take up the pen immediately. Due to many social intercourse and frequent donation to social welfare organizations and faculty and students of Beida, his salary almost fell short of expenditures every month. Sometimes, he even relied on his wife, Huang Zhongyu, to help out with family expenses by selling paintings.

蔡元培一生清廉。他长期在北京任职，却始终没有私房，一直是租住他人房屋。直到晚年仍是如此。他的书籍分放在京沪宁杭等地，没有集中安置的地方。在他70岁寿辰前夕，一些朋友和学生曾经倡议集款为他建一所住宅，得到数百人响应，但因抗日战争的爆发而未能实现。曾任北大教授的王世杰在《追忆蔡元培》一文中写道："蔡先生为公众服务数十年，死后无一间屋，无一寸土，医院药费一千余元，蔡夫人至今尚无法给付，只在那里打算典衣质物以处丧事，衣衾棺木的费用，还是王云五先生代筹的……"

Cai Yuanpei was honest and upright all his life. Though assuming office for a long time in Beijing, he had never had his own private house but rent others' houses. This situation remained the same till his old age. His books were scattered in Beijing, Ningbo and Hangzhou, and there was no such a place for all of them. On the eve of his 70 year-old birthday, some friends and students of him ever proposed to raise money to build a residence for him and this proposal had won responses from several hundred persons, but it was not realized due to the outbreak of anti-Japanese war. In his *Reminiscing Cai Yuanpei*, Wang Shijie, a professor of Beida ever, wrote:"Mr. Cai has served the public for decades, leaving not even a single room, an inch of land, only medical expenses of more than 1,000 silver dollars unpaid after his death. Mrs. Cai has not paid them to date, planning there to pawn clothes and articles for expenses of his coffin and funeral. It was still raised by Mr. Wang Yunwu instead...."

蔡元培重视同友人的社交活动，东堂子胡同蔡寓接待过的社会名流无法统计。胡适曾于1919年9月11日来访，与主人相谈甚欢；周氏兄弟也曾上门求见，如《周作人日记》1920年10月5日载："至东堂子胡同访蔡先生，托买世界语书。"陈独秀更是独往独来，高谈阔论。蔡元培假日常和北大师生去香山卧佛寺一带郊游，有时携友到西四广济寺听讲佛经。朋友间还经常礼尚往来。蔡元培知道周氏兄弟喜好搜集汉碑图案拓本，常花钱购买后赠送。周作人到北大不久，即接到蔡寄送的定州石刻拓本四种，并到蔡寓"观龟甲兽骨文字"。鲁迅在1917年5月21日的日记中记述："夜得蔡先生函并《赞三宝福业碑》、《高归彦造像》、《丰乐七帝二寺邑义等造像》、《苏轼等访象老题记》拓本各二份。"

Cai Yuanpei valued social activities with friends, and received innumerable socialites at his residence in Dongtangzi Alley. Hu Shi ever called on him on September 11, 1919 and had an enjoyable conversation with the host; Zhou brothers ever

1920年6月，蔡元培欢迎法国数学家班乐卫到北京大学讲学。
At No. 75 Dongtangzi Alley, Cai Yuanpei was welcoming Paul Painlevè to Peking University to give lectures.

visited, as recorded in *Zhou Zuoren's Dairy* of October 5, 1920: "I went to Dongtangzi alley to see Mr. Cai and asked for his favor to buy world language books for me." Chen Duxiu also came and went alone even freely, and had hearty talks with Cai. during holidays, Cai often travel to Temple of Recumbent Buddha of fragrant mountain with teachers and students of Beida and sometimes he took friends to Guangji Temple of Xisi to listen to the teaching of Buddhist scriptures. There were often courtesy calls between Cai and his friends. Knowing that Zhou brothers were fond of collecting rubbing of stone stele designs of Han Dynasty, Mr. Cai oftern brought some and gave them to Zhou brothers. Briefly after arrival at Beida, Zhou Zuoren then received four kinds of rubbing of Dingzhou stone inscriptions posted by Cai Yuanpei and went to his residence to watch inscriptions on oracle bones. According to dairy of Lu Xun on May 21, 1917, "I received the letter of Cai at night accomplished by two copies of rubbing of *Stele of Praise of Merit and Virtue of Three Jewels*, *Statute Building by Gao Guiyan*, *Statute Building by Yiyi Disciples in Two Fengle Seven Emperors' Temples*, and *Inscriptions on Su Shi's Visit to Master Xiang*."

蔡元培夫妇在家待客是有选择的。他在《祭亡妻黃仲玉》一文中称妻子"对于北京妇女以酒食赌博相征逐，或假公益之名以鸷声气而因缘为利者，尤慎避之，不敢与往来。常克勤克俭以养我之廉，以端正子女之习惯"。据沈迈士回忆："有一次我在蔡先生家和他谈话，来了一位客人，提了礼品求见蔡先生。先生严辞谢绝，并把礼物推出大门之外。"

 Cai Yuanpei couple was selective in treating guests at home. In his "In Memory of Deceased Wife Huang Zhongyu", he spoke of his wife "For Beijing women who competed in wining, dining and gambling or sought for interests as ducks in the name of public welfare, she avoided them cautiously in particular and dared not to associate with them. She was always diligent and economic to encourage my honesty and rectify habits of children." As recalled by Shen Maishi, "One time, I was talking with Mr. Cai at his home. A guest carrying gifts came and asked to see Mr. Cai. Mr. Cai turned him down sternly and pushed the gifts out of his door."

蔡元培工作之余喜欢写对联，好书法，言明"要将书法作为美育的一个重要内容"。任教育总长时，他曾自题一对联自勉，并悬挂于书室，联曰："都无作官意；惟有读书声。"蔡元培还为蔡元康书写对联云："行不得则反求诸己；躬自厚而薄责于人。"意思是说，事情进行不下去时要在自身找原因，多反省自己而不要刻薄责备别人。他的书房挂了一幅自己的画像，上面题写"其为人也，发愤忘食，乐以忘忧，亦不知老之将至"；他的书桌也有自己写的横帧"学不厌，教不倦"，透露出主人处事治学的精神境界。毛子水在《对于蔡元培的一些回忆》中讲到一件趣事。某

蔡元培手稿
The manuscript of Cai Yuanpei

次，钱玄同问道："蔡先生，前清考翰林，都要字写得很好的才能考中，先生的字写得这样蹩脚，怎样能够考得翰林？"蔡先生笑答："我也不知道，大概那时正风行黄山谷（黄庭坚）字体的缘故吧！"马叙伦在《石屋续沈》中评价蔡元培的书法："其入翰林也，试者得其卷大喜，评其文盛称之，而于其书法则曰'牛鬼蛇神'。""牛鬼蛇神"一词指蔡元培书法兼容多种书派，本身不矫揉造作，宁丑勿媚，古拙奇朴，体现个性。

In his spare time, Cai Yuanpei loved writing couplets and calligraphy, stating explicitly "to take calligraphy as an important content of aesthetic education". When he was the education minister, he ever composed a couplet to encourage himself and hung it in his study. The couplet reads "No will for official position, admiring sound of reading alone". Cai Yuanpei also wrote a couplet for Cai Yuankang, reading "When you are not successful in what you are doing, try to look back into yourself; he who requires much from himself and little from others will keep himself from being the object of resentment". It means when one can not go on with something, he should turn to himself for reasons, making self-examination instead of reproaching others. He hung a portrait of himself in his study, on which saying "A person shall be one that pursue knowledge so as to forget to eat, so happy that as to forget worries and did not realize of his coming old age."; his desk also bore a horizontal frame written by himself, "Study hard and never feel contented, and never be tired of teaching others", revealing his spiritual realm of dealing with people and scholarship. Mao Zishui mentioned an interesting story in "Some Memories of Cai Yuanpei". One time, Qian Xuantong asked: "Mr. Cai, in the early Qing dynasty, only those capable of wonderful handwriting could be enrolled. How can you, with such poor handwriting, be admitted as a member of Hanlin Academy?" Mr. Cai replied with a smile: "I don't know either. Maybe, Huang Shangu's style of handwriting was prevailing at that time." In *Record in the Stone House*, Ma Xulun commented the handwriting of Cai Yuanpei, "When he competed for Hanli, the examiner was much delighted to see his test paper, praised his article, but said his handwriting as 'Monsters and Demons'." "Monsters and Demons" means that the handwriting of Cai Yuanpei combined various writing styles, being natural and not affected itself, rather ugly than subservience, clumsy, unusual and delicate, a manifestation of his personality.

蔡元培言谈中不乏幽默。蔡元培常用的笔名有"周子余"，友人问其故，蔡元培笑答：周、蔡原为一家，不闻蔡亦出自姬姓乎？ 当年他到总统府向袁世凯当面辞教育总长职时，袁对他说："我代表四万万人留君。"蔡元培说："元培亦对四万万人之代表而辞职。"

Cai's remarks were also found humorous. One of his common pen-names was Zhou Ziyu. A friend asked him the reason for choosing that name, he answered with a smile, "Zhou and Cai were formerly from the same family, don't you know that Cai was also originated from the surname Ji?" In that year, he went to the presidential palace to resign his post of education minister in person before Yuan Shikai, Yuan told him, "I keep you back on behalf of the 400 million people." Cai replied, "Yuanpei resign on behalf of the 400 million people."

蔡元培自1917年入职北京大学至1927年底离开，共有10年半的时间。他曾自谦地说："综计我居北京大学校长的名义，十年有半，而实际在校办事，不过五年有半，一经回忆，不胜惭悼。"然而，事实已经证明，这10年是北大历史上生机勃勃、辉煌灿烂的10年，也是蔡元培生命历程中光彩夺目、建树最大的10年。这期间，北大完成了历史性的变革，成为国人瞩目、青年向往的新文化运动的中心，五四运动的发祥地，在中国传播马克思主义和发展教育科学文化的基地，为中国近现代历史的发展作出了不可磨灭的贡献。这一切都是同蔡元培的筚路蓝缕、革故鼎新分不开的。纵观蔡元培立德、立功、立言的不朽人生，当属登泰山而小天下，富贵于我为浮云，人不知而不愠，朝闻道夕死可矣，风乎舞雩咏而归，道不行乘桴浮于海的儒家处世心境。时间相隔越久远，蔡元培这位新文化运动的护法人就越加显露出其儒家本色。与之神往，如沐春风。

There was a total of ten and a half years since Cai Yuanpei took his post in Beida in 1917 to his departure at the end of 1927. He ever said humbly: "Since I held the position of chancellor of Beida, it has been a total of

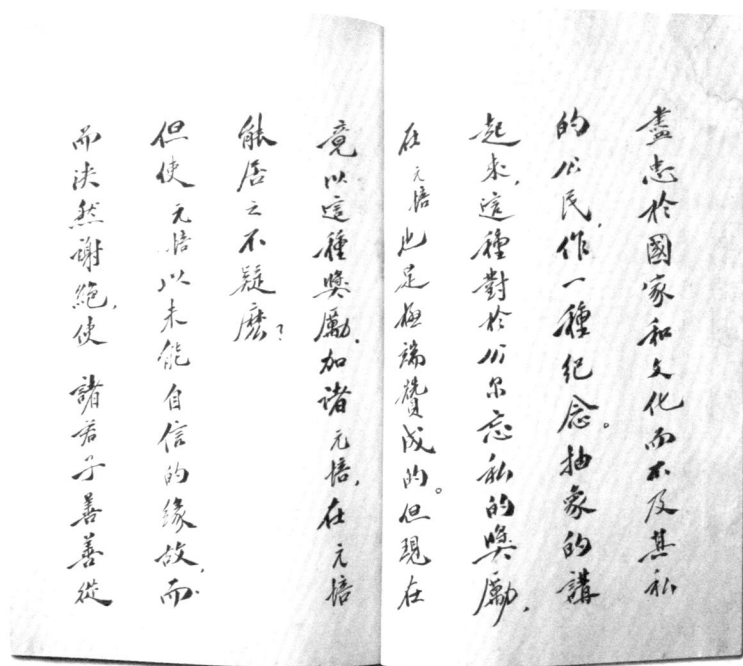

蔡元培手稿
The manuscript of Cai Yuanpei

10 and a half years, while the total years I actually worked for it amounted no more than 5 years. Whenever I recall that experience, I feel quite ashamed." However, the facts have proven that these ten years were the most vibrant and splendid 10 years of Beida's history, also the most dazzling and fruitful 10 years of Cai Yuanpei throughout his life. During his service, Beida had completed its historic transformation, becoming the center of New Culture Movement focused by the people and admired by youth, the origin of May 4th Movement, a base for disseminating Marxism and developing science and culture in China, and had made indelible contributions to the development of modern Chinese history. All these were indispensable to the hardships Cai Yuanpei underwent and his reform of Beida. Looking on the immortal life of Cai Yuanpei known for his virtue, achievements and speech, his attitudes shall belong to the Confucian philosophy of life, known as "the world is dwarfed when seen from Taishan", "riches and honors are to me as the floating clouds", "to remain unsoured even though one's merits are unrecognized by others", "if one learns the truth in the morning, one would never regret dying the same evening", "enjoy the breeze among the rain altars, and return home singing", and "my doctrines make no way, I will get upon a raft, and float about on the sea". The farer the time, Cai Yuanpei, the protector of New Culture Movement, shows even more his true attribute of Confucianism. One feels like bathing in the spring breeze when having spiritual communication with him.

京城旧宅 历史记忆

谈到蔡元培，自然就要提到他在北京的故居。

Speaking of Cai Yuanpei, it is natural to mention his old residence in Beijing.

蔡元培在北京居住的时间并不太长，主要是1917年至1923年担任北京大学校长那段时间。那期间他曾多次出国，而且在北京住过的地方也有多处，而后来将他在东堂子胡同的住处定为其故居，有着十分特殊的意义，那就是因为它与那场震惊中外的五四运动有着直接的关联。

Cai Yuanpei didn't stay in Beijing for a very long time, mainly the period when he served as the chancellor of Beida from 1917 to 1923. During that period, he went abroad many times, and he ever lived in a number of residences. It is of special significance to decide his residence in Dongtangzi Alley as his old residence, as it was directly related to the world-shocking May 4th Movement.

东堂子胡同是北京东单北大街路东的一条胡同，胡同不太宽，也不曲折，胡同自西向东连通了东单北大街与朝阳门南小街，虽居闹市，却很安静。这条胡同在明代称堂子胡同，有近800年的历史，当属北京最老的胡同之一了。清时改称东堂子胡同。"堂子"一词，在明清时为苏沪一带妓院的俗称；后来伶人名角的寓所和私房科班也称为堂子。北京本有"东贵西阔"的说法，因为文官每天上早朝须经紫禁城东华门出入，所以多在东城就近择宅，一些艺妓戏班便也云集东城。据明末清初周筼《析津日记》云："京师黄华坊，有东院，有本司胡同。所谓本司者，盖即教坊司也。又有勾栏胡同、演乐胡同，其近处还有马姑娘胡同、宋姑娘胡同、粉子胡同。"明朝的教坊司负责宫廷音乐与戏曲活动，官妓院也归其管辖。上述胡同紧邻东堂子胡同以北，可见这一带曾经歌舞升平，为明清两代京官娱乐、社交场所。

Dongtangzi alley is at the east side of Dongdan North Street. The alley is not so wide, nor is winding, it connects

Dongdan North Street and Chaoyangmen Nanxiaojie from west to east. Though located in the bustling area, it is very quiet. This alley was named Tangzi Alley in the Ming Dynasty and has a history of nearly 800 years, belonging to one of the oldest alleys in Beijing. It was renamed as East Tangzi Alley in the Qing Dynasty. Tangzi was the nickname for brothels of Suzhou and Shanghai during Ming and Qing dynasties; later the residence and private training classes of famous mummers were also referred to as Tangzi. There had been a saying in Beijing "noble in the east and rich in the west", as civil officials mostly chose their residence in the east city as they must pass

20世纪初东单附近旧街景
The old street landscape near Dongdan at the early of 20th century

through Donghuamen of the forbidden city for attending the morning court, some mummers and theatrical troupes also gathered in the east city. According to *Xijin Dairy* by Zhou Yun who lived in Late Ming Dynasty to Early Qing Dynasty: Huhuangfang of the capital city has east yard and the alley of our own department. The so-called our own department is probably Academy of Music. There are also Goulan alley, Yanle alley, and Maguniang alley, Songguniang alley and Fenzi alley nearby. The Academy of Music of the Ming Dynasty took charge of court music and operatic activities, official brothels were also under its jurisdiction. The above-mentioned alleys are close to the north of Dongtangzi Alley. It can be seen that this area was ever the place of singing and dancing and places for entertainment and social activities of capital officials of Ming and Qing dynasty.

20世纪初东单附近旧街景
The old street landscape near Dongdan at the early of
20th century

到了晚清，东堂子胡同成为总理各国事务衙门，也即后来的北洋政府外交部所在。东部设有被称为"新教育之肇端"的中国最早的外语教学机构京师同文馆，1900年遭义和团拳民进驻的毁坏，1903年被并入京师大学堂改名京师译学馆，同年迁入北河沿新址（即现在民政部、最高人民检察院所在地），其旧址很可能修缮后继续使用。若此，东堂子胡同便是蔡元培所熟悉的地方。蔡元培在《我在北京大学的经历》中记述："北京大学的名称，是从民国元年起的，民元以前，名为京师大学堂，包括师范馆、仕学馆等，而译学馆亦为其一部。我在民元前六年，曾任译学馆教员，讲授国文及西洋史，是为我在北大服务之第一次。"

Up to late Qing dynasty, Dongtangzi alley became the office for handling affairs of various countries, namely the location of Ministry of Foreign Affairs of Beiyang government later; Capital Foreign Language Institute, the earliest foreign language teaching institution of China, also called the "beginning of new education", was set in the east and was destroyed by the garrison of boxers of Yihetuan Group in 1900. In 1903, it was incorporated into Imperial Capital University and renamed as Capital Translation Institute. In the same year, it was relocated to the new site of Beiheyan (the location of the present Ministry of Civil Affairs, the Supreme People's Procuratorate), its old site might be renovated for continued use. If so, Dongtangzi alley was the place most familiar to Cai Yuanpei. In "My Experience in Peking University", Cai Yuanpei related: "The name of Peking university was given at the first year of Republic of China; before that, it was called Capital Metropolitan University, including faculty of education, school for administration, and others, while Translation Institute was also a part of it. In the first 6 years of Republic of China, I was ever a teacher of the translation institute and taught Chinese and western history. It was my first time providing service in Beida."

东堂子胡同西侧对面就是煤渣胡同。民国元年（1912年）2月27日孙中山派遣的由蔡元培、宋教仁等组成的专使团，就住在煤渣胡同由贵胄法政学堂改成的招待所。专使团的任务是敦促袁世凯离京到南京就任总统。袁世凯不愿离开北京，指使部下发动兵变，乱兵闯进专使团的驻地，搜人、抢劫、放火，将专使团的文件、行李抢劫一空。蔡元培等人翻墙逃脱后建议南京方面妥协，最终同意袁世凯在北京就任总统。

The west opposite of Dongtangzi alley is Meizha Alley. On February 27 of the first year of the ROC (1912), a special delegation assigned by Sun Yat-Sen made up of Cai Yuanpei and Song Jiaoren just lived in the hostel of Meizha alley renovated from Royal School of Politics and Law. The task of the special delegation was to urge Yuan Shikai to leave Beijing and assume the presidency in Nanjing. Because Yuan Shikai was unwilling to leave Beijing, he ordered his subordinates to launch a mutiny. The solders on rampage broke in the site of the delegates, searching people, robbing, setting fire, and looted all documents and luggage of the delegates. After escape by climbing over the wall, Cai Yuanpei and others suggested Nanjing side to compromise and Yuan Shikai was finally approved to take the post of president in Beijing.

北京大学校长蔡子民肖像

东堂子胡同75号院，旧时的门牌是东堂子胡同33号，原为东、西各三进的普通四合院落，原大门在中间，现分为75、77号两个院落。蔡元培寓此时，将一进院的5间南房（俗称倒座）安置仆人和门房。二进院3间北房为蔡元培的孩子居住，前有走廊，左右各带1间耳房作厨房和储藏间，东、西厢房各3间为亲友客房，南房4间作为会客的客厅，第三进北房5间为蔡元培的卧室和书房，带走廊。如同北京其他的老宅院一样，院落地面是方砖墁地，院中植有树木，春天花满枝头，冬天则枝叶凋零，居住院中，便能感受到京城的四时风雨。

北京大学预科职员通讯录
The address book of preparatory staffs of Peking University

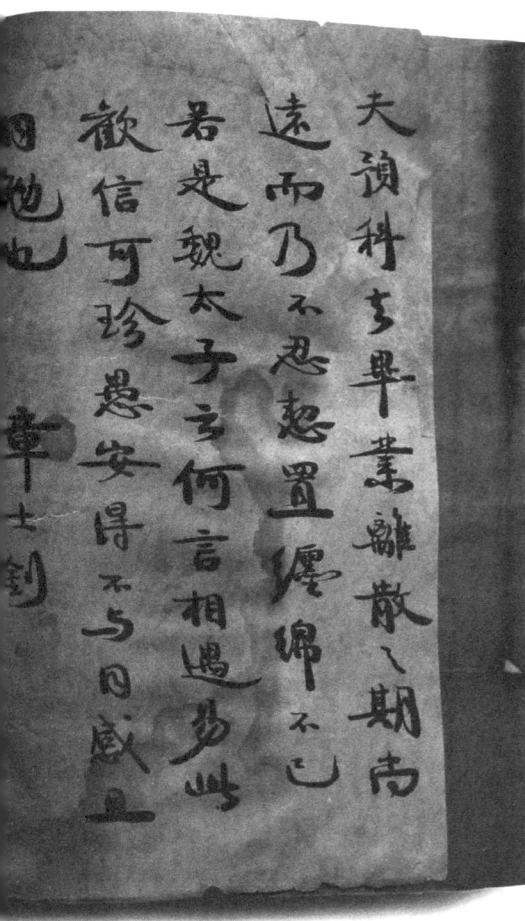

东堂子胡同西口
The west of Dongtangzi alley
故居修缮前鸟瞰图
The aerial view of the former residence
before repair

No. 75 yard of Dongtangzi alley, whose doorplate was No. 33 in old times, was originally an ordinary courtyard comprising triple yards in both east and west. Its entrance door was in the middle at first and now is divided into No. 75 and No. 77 yards. When residing there, Cai Yuanpei assigned the 5 south-facing rooms (nicknamed as reverse seat) of the first courtyard for servants and doormen. The 3 south-facing rooms of the 2nd courtyard were residence of Cai Yuanpei's children, with a corridor in front. There was a side room on each side as the kitchen and storehouse, the wing rooms,

three on each side, were guestrooms for relatives and friends, the 4 north-facing rooms were the living room for receiving guests. The 5 south-facing rooms of the 3rd courtyard with a corridor were the bedroom and study of Cai Yuanpei. As other old yards of Beijing, the ground was paved with square bricks and trees are planted in the yard. The plants are dotted with flowers in spring while withered and bare in winter, living in the yard, one can feel the seasonal changes of Beijing.

修缮前的故居大门
The gate of the former residence before repair

修缮前故居前院倒座房
The south house of the former residence before repair

东堂子胡同75号，记录了蔡元培的一段生活轨迹，截留了蔡元培与五四运动那一时期的岁月，作为历史的见证，东堂子胡同75号将被人们永远记住。蔡元培自1923年1月离开北京后就很少再回来了。岁月更替，世事变迁，这个原本再普通不过的75号院因了20世纪初那场轰轰烈烈的五四爱国运动，在特定时期产生深远的历史影响而变得不再平常了。1986年6月，北京市东城区人民政府将该院作为"蔡元培故居"公布为文物保护单位。

No. 75 of Dongtangzi alley witnessed a period of life of Cai Yuanpei and recorded the days of Cai Yuanpei and May 4th Movement. As the witness of history, No. 75 of Dongtangzi alley will be remembered by people forever. Cai seldom returned after he left Beijing in January 1923. Time elapses and things change, No. 75 yard, which was originally ordinary to the bone, produced profound historic impact during the special period and became no more usual because of the spectacular May 4th Movement of the last century. In June 1986, People's Government of Dongcheng District of Beijing announced the yard as "Former Residence of Cai Yuanpei" and a cultural relics site for protection.

修缮前故居前院倒座房
The south house of the former residence before repair

由于历史的原因，蔡元培故居几十年来一直被当成普通民居使用，属于东城区房管所直管公房。及至上世纪90年代末期，75号院里已经住进了14户人家，使得原本就拥挤的小院更加不堪重负。人为的损坏和年久失修，大面积的承重墙已出现很多的裂缝，加上诸多的临时搭建，四合院早已破旧不堪，全然看不到一丝故居当年的格局和影子了，接待社会各界参观更是无从提起。

Due to historical reason, the former residence of Cai Yuanpei has been used as ordinary houses for decades and has been a public house directly under the jurisdiction of Real Estate Management Bureau of Dongcheng District. By the end of 1990s, No. 75 yard had been jammed with 14 households, making the small crowded yard even more overburdened. Many cracks have appeared on large areas of the bearing wall due to human damages and long time disrepair. This, in addition to many temporary buildings, makes the yard dilapidated and in tatters, without even a trace of the patterns and images of Cai's days, not to mention of receiving guests for visit.

修缮前故居前院到中院夹道
The alley in the central yard before repair

修缮前故居中院临建房
The temporary house in the central yard before repair
修缮前故居中院北房与东厢房
The north house and the east wing in the central yard before repair

修缮前故居中院倒座房

The south house in the central yard before repair

东堂子胡同75号院

No. 75 Yard in Dongtangzihutong Alleyway

蔡元培故居的前世今生
The Past and Present of
Cai Yuanpei's Former Residence

目录

Contents

The Present

1

1998年北京市政府启动了金宝街旧城危房拆迁改造项目，正是因为这个项目的启动，才使得对蔡元培故居的保护和修缮工作提到政府的议事日程中来，让这个历经百年风雨的小院有机会以其原有的面貌向世人开放，真正承担起教育后人启迪后世的责任。

Beijing Municipal Government launched a program of demolishment and reconstruction of dilapidated and unsafe houses on Jinbao Street in 1998. It was due to this program that the protection and repair of the former residence of Cai Yuanpei was brought into the agenda of the government. Thanks to this opportunity, this yard that has undergone a century's ups and downs can take on a new look, be open to the public, and shoulder in a true sense the opportunity of educating and edifying later generations.

1 时任北京市主管副市长汪光焘（右一）亲临故居视察（右三：富华国际集团总裁赵勇）
Wang Guangtao, deputy mayor of Peking, was inspecting the former residence.
2 富华国际集团主席陈丽华与时任东城区区长陈平研究规划方案
Chan Laiwa, Chairman of Fu Wah International Group, and Chen Ping, the district mayor of Dongcheng District, were researching the planning scheme.

金宝街属于北京市市政带危改项目，被列为北京市及东城区的重点工程项目之一，是1998年北京市政府赴港招商的签约项目，目的是扩大王府井商圈。金宝街的整体规划东至朝内南小街，西至东单北大街，南至东堂子胡同，北至干面胡同。这样可以把王府井大街和东二环路直接相连，使王府井大街除了南北两头外又多了一条和二环连接的通道，以分流往来的车辆，缓解王府井的交通紧张状况。作为市政带危改工程，需要对金宝街道路两侧进行危旧房改造。和以往由政府修路的市政工程不同的是，这一项目是由开发商投资修路、解决居民拆迁费用，政府给予开发商道路两侧开发权及配套优惠政策。这种开发模式在北京还是第一次采用，在全国也属首创。

Jinbao Street, belonging to "housing reform drives reform of unsafe houses" project of Beijing municipality, was listed as one of the major projects of Beijing and Dongcheng district. It was a contracted project of Beijing Municipal Government to Hong Kong for business invitation in order to expand the business circle of Wang Fujing in 1998. According to the overall plan of Jinbao Street, it extends to Chaonei Nanxiaojie in the east, to Dongdan North Street and Dongsi South Street in the west, to Dongtangzi alley in the south, and to Ganmian alley in the north. Thus, Wangfujing Street and east 2nd ring road can be linked directly, enabling another passage connected with the 2nd ring road besides its south and north ends. As a result, the traffic can be diverted and the traffic pressure of Wang Fujing be relieved. As a "housing reform drives reform of unsafe houses" project, it needed to renovate the dilapidated and dangerous houses on both sides of Jinbao Street. Different from past municipal engineering of the government such as road construction, the developer was

富华国际集团领导与北京市东城区政府的领导商讨修缮方案。
Leaders of Fu Wah International Group and Dongcheng District were discussing the repair plan.

to make investment to construct roads and reimburse the relocation fees, the government provided the developer rights of developing two sides of the road and ancillary preferential policies. Such a development pattern was adopted for the first time in Beijing, and was also an initiative in China.

北京市委市政府高度重视金宝街市政改造及危改工程的建设，突出强调改造中对北京古都传统风貌的保护，并明确指示对工程中涉及的历史文物要制定抢救性措施。为此，市领导和东城区政府以及作为开发者的富华国际集团共同与规划部门，文物专家等多次研究、论证、修改和调整方案，对

该地区留存的历史文物采取了积极可行的抢救措施，并规划建设一片充分体现北京古都传统风貌的四合院小区。

Beijing Municipal Committee and Government attached great importance to the municipal improvement and the renovation of dilapidated houses of Jinbao Street, highlighted the protection of traditional outlook of ancient Beijing, and gave explicit directions to the formulation of rescuing measures for the historic relics involved in the project. Therefore, the municipal leaders, Dongcheng district government and the developer Fu Wah International Group studied, discussed, modified and adjusted the plans for many times together with planning and cultural relics experts, adopted active and feasible rescue measures for the historic relics preserved in such area, and planed to build a courtyard community fully reflecting traditional style and features of ancient Beijing (i.e. plot 7 of Jinbao Street).

1 集团总裁赵勇（右二）与时任东城区区长陈平（右四）在现场研究修缮方案。

Chiu Yung, the president of Fu Wah International Group and Chen Ping, the district mayor of Dongcheng District were researching the repair plan.

2 故居修缮现场，工人把故居的砖瓦小心拆下并分门别类的保存。

On the scene of repairing the former residence, workers were carefully disassembling tiles from the former residence, sorting out and preserving them.

3、4 故居修缮现场，"墩接"前原状

The scene of repairing the former residence, the original outlook before "Dun Jie"

位于东堂子胡同75号院的蔡元培故居和金宝街的开发是整体相联的。故居不仅是金宝街的一个文物保护单位，也是整个金宝街的一个亮点。开发金宝街，不但体现了富华国际集团的经济实力，更是一次爱国之举，也是一次创新之举。富华国际集团主席陈丽华女士和集团总裁赵勇先生对此高度重视，专门组织各方面专家考察论证，制定修缮方案。并与北京市政府、市文物局、市规划委等多个部门进行磋商研讨。可以说，蔡元培故居的保护和修复是一个历史性的过程，在这个过程中，作为投资方的富华国际集团经历了对遗址保护的规划、独立存在以及之后修复和评价等多个阶段，付出了极大的心智和努力。

The former residence of Cai Yuanpei located at No.75 yard of

Dongtangzi alley was integrated as a whole with the development of Jinbao Street. Mr. Cai's former residence is not only an unit of cultural relics protection of Jinbao Street, but also a highlight of the whole Jinbao Street. To develop Jinbao Street not only shows the economic strength of Fu Wah International Group, but also a patriotic and innovative action. Ms. Chan Laiwa, a CPPCC Member and chairman of Fu Wah International Group, and Mr. Chiu Yung, president of Fu Wah Group, attached great importance to this, specially organized various experts for survey and demonstration, and worked out repair plan. They also discussed and consulted with Beijing Municipal Government, Beijing Municipal Administration of Cultural Heritage, Beijing Municipal Commission of Urban Planning, and others. It can be said that the protection and restoration of Cai Yuanpei's former residence was a historic process, during which the investor, Fu Wah International Group, experienced many phases such as the planning of the site protection,

修缮后的故居全貌
The panorama of the former residence after repair

independent existence, renovation and evaluation thereafter, and paid substantial attention and efforts.

在规划之初，对于是否原址保护专家组一直存在两种观点：一部分人认为应该原地保留、修复；一部分人认为异地保护为好，即将故居拆建于原址向东200米处，即规划中的7号四合院区。在进行过多次论证后，最终决定原址保护！以最大程度还原历史本来。随后，原址保护如何实施又成为大家讨论的焦点。是独立保留还是和整体规划联成一体保留？在最初的设想中，计划在金宝街五号地块，即现在的励骏酒店的主楼西南角挑高15米探出一平台，平台下面即是故居原址，在原址处

重建，四周辅以玻璃幕墙保护，使之成为一个室内的博物馆。这样，既在整体上做到了原地保护故居，又与酒店主楼建筑合为一体，而15米以上的空间又可以合理利用，使其商业价值得到充分的延展。这看起来是个两全其美的构想，然而在几经论证后，这一设想首先被集团主席陈丽华女士否决了。

At the beginning of the planning, expert panel for the protection of the original site held two different opinions: some believed that the original site should be preserved and renovated while others believed that the preservation of another place was better, that is the old residence should be demolished and rebuilt at the site 200 meters east from the original site, namely the No. 7 courtyard area in the planning. After rounds of deliberations, it was finally decided to protect the original site so as to restore the original history to the largest extent. Afterwards, how to implement the protection of the original site became again the focus of the discussion. Should it preserved independently or preserved together with

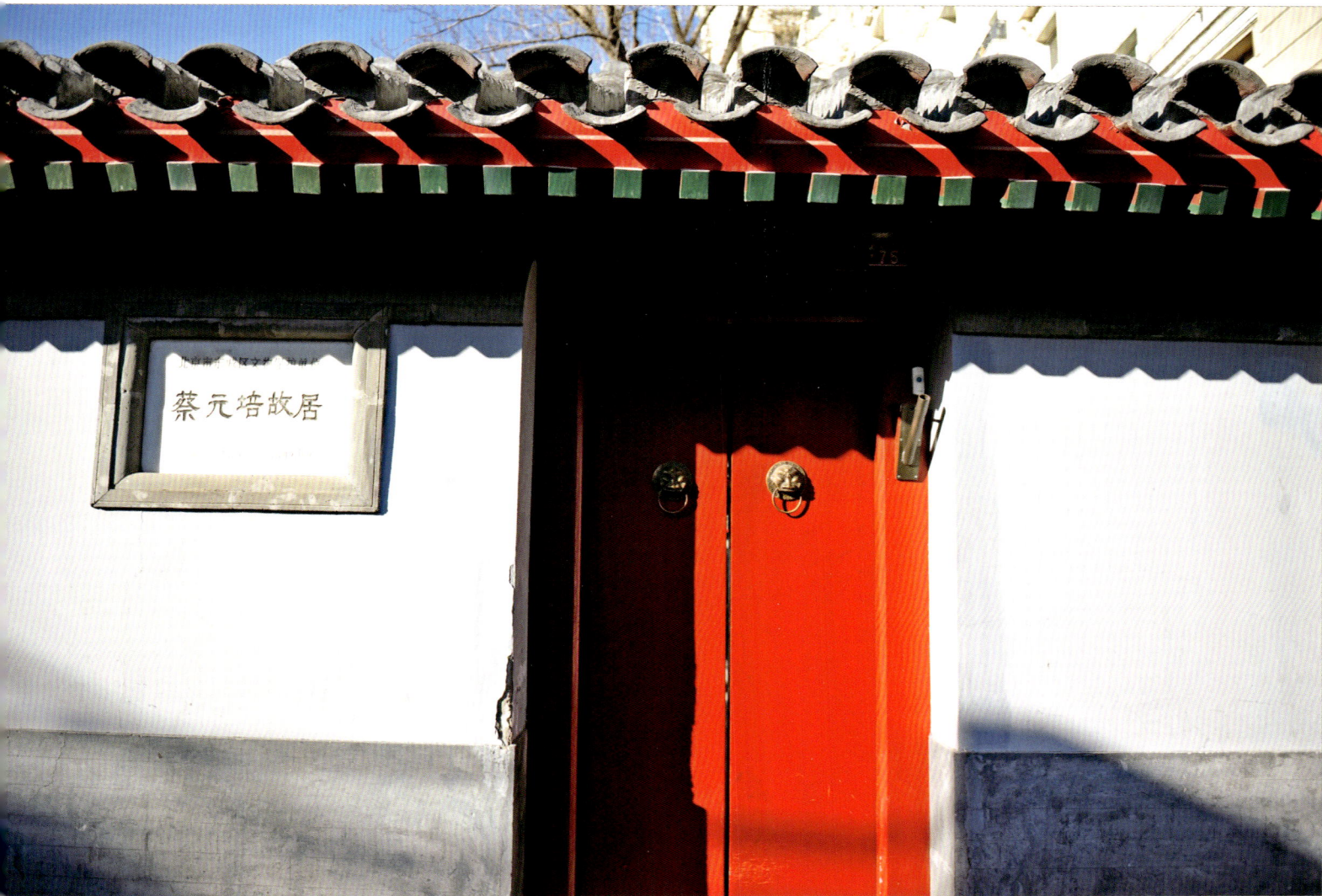

修缮后的故居大门
The gate of the former residence after repair

the overall plan as a whole? In the initial assumption, it planned to erect a 18-meter platform at No. 5 plot of Jinbao Street, namely the southwest corner of the main building of the current Legandale Hotel. Under the platform was just the original site of Cai's former residence. Rebuilding was to be carried out at the original site, glass walls were to be mounted all around for protection to make it an indoor museum. In this way, the old residence could not only be protected at the original site, but also integrated with the main building of the hotel. In addition, the space above 15 meters was available for rational use, making

its commercial value fully extended. It seemed that such an idea made the best of both world. However, it was denied first by Chan Laiwa, chairman of the group, after several rounds of argumentation.

陈丽华这一传奇人物是满族正黄旗后裔，从小生长在北京的她有着极其深厚的老北京情结。当年不惜重金打造中国紫檀博物馆，旨在保护和传承中国传统的檀雕技艺和中国明清家具制作工艺。现在投资金宝街，其目的也不仅仅只是想在这寸土寸金的地方盖几座现代化的高楼，她骨子里难舍的故土情结注定了她要在这块黄金宝地上有一番不寻常的作为。因此，在蔡元培故居的保护问题上，她有自己的想法：保护就要彻底保护，不要怕花钱，从保护国家文物、历史遗迹的角度出发，让出一部分商业用地，使蔡元培故居以其原本的面貌，独立地融于周边的环境当中，通天透地。这一举动再一次体现了富华国际集团高度的文物保护意识和丰厚的企业文化内涵。

Chan Laiwa, a legendary figure, is a descendant of Plain Yellow Banner of Man Nationality. Brought up in

修缮后的故居屋檐墙脊
The eave and ridge of the former residence
after repair

Beijing, she has a deep emotional complex for old Beijing. In the past, she spared no expense to build the China Red Sandalwood Museum in order to protect and inherit traditional Chinese sandalwood carving techniques and manufacturing techniques of Ming and Qing furniture; now, she makes investment to Jinbao Street so as to not only build several modern high buildings on the place an inch of which is as expensive as an inch of gold, but also to achieve some unusual results on this golden land because of her loving complex for the hometown. Therefore, as to the protection of Cai Yuanpei's old residence, she had her own idea:

1

a thorough protection of it was needed if it was to be protected, money should not be spared. From the angle of protecting national cultural relics and historic sites, a part of commercial land was to be let. Therefore, Cai Yuanpei's old residence in its original outlook can be independently melt in the nearby surroundings, standing penetrating heaven and earth. Such an action showed again Fu Wah's high awareness of cultural relics protection and the rich connotations of its corporate culture.

在确定原址翻建、力争保存文物实物的故居修缮方案后，富华国际集团不惜在寸金之地投入大笔资金，独自承担起毫无经济回报的拆迁和建设费用，搬迁了院内的14户居民，按照拆迁政策改善了这些居民的住房条件，拆除了违章建筑，实现了文物腾退，为故居的保护利用创造了条件。

After determination of the renovation plan of Cai Yuanpei's old residence as "rebuilding at the original

1 修缮后的故居前院倒座房
The south house in front yard of the former residence after repair
2、3 修缮后的故居前院到中院之间的过道
The alley from the front yard to the central yard in the former residence after repair

site and renovating the old into old", Fu Wah International Group didn't spare a large amount of funds in the land of "one inch costs one inch gold", shouldered independently the relocation and construction expenses without any economic return, relocated the 14 households in the yard, improved the living conditions of the residents in line with the relocation policy, demolished the illegal construction, vacated the space for cultural relics, and created conditions for the protection and use of the old residence.

2007年7月，在北京市及东城区两级文物部门的指导下，蔡元培故居修复工程正式启动。富华国际集团总裁赵勇先生亲自担任工程领导小组组长，集团分管房地产事务的王守元总经理不顾年事已高亲自监督工程的进度。修复施工方案委托北京古建设计研究所精心设计，由北京房修二公司古建工程公司具体施工。为更好地还原故居的时代特色，集团还聘请了故宫古建老专家王仲杰先生、中国古建筑学会施工专业委员会主任刘大可先生亲临现场指导。

In July 2007, under the direction of cultural heritage administrations of Beijing and Dongcheng District, the restoration project of Cai Yuanpei's former residence was formally launched. Mr. Chiu Yung, president of Fu Wah International Group, acted in person as the leader of the project leading group, Wan Shouyuan, general manager of the group in charge of real estate affairs, supervised in person the progresses of the project despite his old age. The delicate design of the restoration and construction plan was entrusted to Beijing Research Institute of Design of Ancient Buildings, and was implemented by Beijing No.2 House Building &

修缮后的故居中院
The central yard of the former residence after repair

Ancient Architectural Engineering Co., Ltd. For a better restoration of the time features of the old residence, the group also engaged Mr. Wang Zhongjie, an old expert in ancient building of the Palace Museum, and Mr. Liu Dake, director of Construction Specialty Committee of China Ancient Architecture Society, came to the site in person for direction.

蔡元培故居的修复不同于一般的四合院建造，要做到按照历史原状恢复和修缮，就一定要尽可能多的使用原有的砖瓦及梁架结构，所以在修复之前，特意请老专家们对施工人员进行了故居保护培训。被拆下来的一砖一瓦，

东堂子胡同75号院 No. 75 Yard in Dongtangzi Hutong Alleyway

修缮后的故居中院
The central yard of the former residence after repair

都分门别类的码放好，再重新用作修复故居的建筑材料；用旧修旧，原汁原味地还原民居的历史旧貌，做到了真正意义上"不改变原状"。例如，对故居木质梁柱的修复，不能简单的用新木进行修补，而是采取一种叫做"墩接"的技术来进行复原，以保证原貌的再现。忆起当年修复时的点点滴滴，陈丽华动情地说："为了完整如旧地保留原貌，我们精心收集了拆迁下来的老瓦，用纸一片片包好，统一归集起来，编上号，重建时再一一对应。"就连屋檐上的如意形滴水、屋前台阶的条石、窗棂下的大开条砖等，都是遍寻京城各拆迁工地淘来的。个中辛苦，也只有日夜辛勤忙碌的他们最为清楚了。

The restoration of Cai Yuanpei's old residence was different from

1、2 修缮后的故居新添加的长廊
The newly-added long corridor of the former residence after repair

3 修缮后的故居后院全貌
The panorama of the back yard of former residence after repair

1

the building of ordinary courtyards. To repair the old into old, the original bricks, tilts and girders should be used as much as possible. Therefore, old experts were specially invited to provide trainings on protection of the old residence for the constructors before the restoration. Every brick and tilt dismantled was assorted and placed well to be reused as the building materials of the old residence; repairing the old with old materials restored the authentic historic outlook of the old residence. For example, as to the repair of the wooden girders of the old residence, the constructors could not simply repair them with new wood, but used a technique of "replace rotten foot of a wooden column" for restoration in order to guarantee the recurrence of its original outlook. When recalling the bits of memories then, Chan Laiwa said emotionally, "In order to fully restore the original outlook, we delicately collected the old tiles dismantled and wrapped each of them with papers, gathered them in a unified way and placed numbers on them for matching at time of rebuilding."

1 修缮后的故居后院全貌
The panorama of the back yard of former residence after repair

2、3 修缮后的故居后门全貌
The panorama of the back door of former residence after repair

Even the ruyi-shaped dripper on the eaves, the stripe stone of the step in front of the house, large stripe bricks under the window ridge were all found by searching all relocation sites throughout Beijing. As to the hardships, no one knew better than themselves who busied day and night then.

蔡元培故居修复工程得到北京市各级政府领导的高度关注，时任北京市主管副市长的汪光焘同志亲临现场考察，并指派专人调查考证，并亲自组织专家进行保护方案的研讨，市区文委也直接介入参与研讨，并对之后的展陈等一系列工作给予了强有力的支持。

026 东堂子胡同75号院 No. 75 Yard in Dongtangzihutong Alleyway

金宝街夜景效果图
The panorama of Jinbao Street

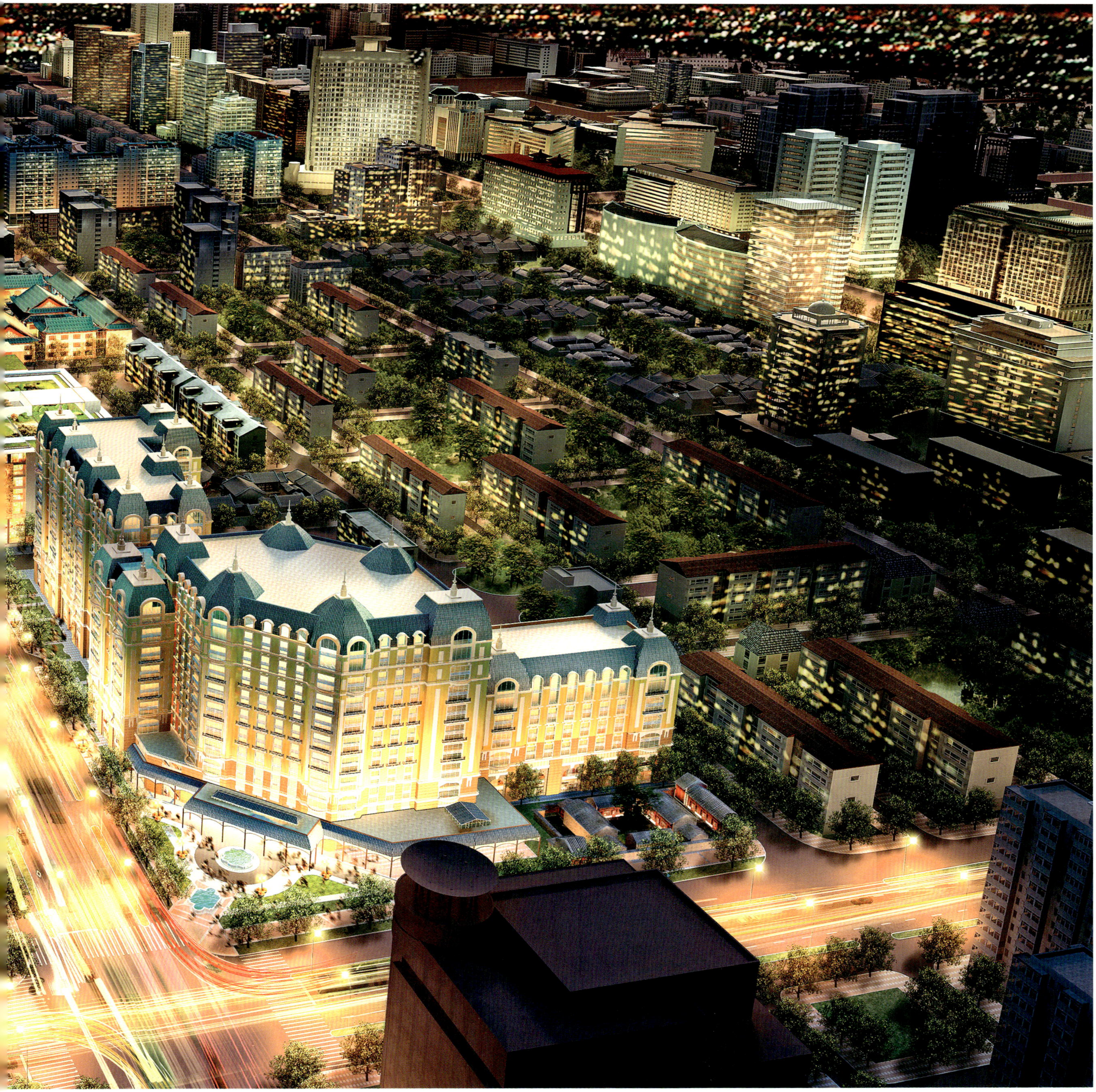

修缮后的故居全貌
The panorama of the former residence after repair

蔡元培故居的昔日与今生 The Past and Present at Cai Yuanpei's Former Residence

The restoration of Cai Yuanpei's old residence received much attention from government leaders at various levels of Beijing. Wang Guangtao, deputy mayor of Beijing, went to the site in person for survey, assigned special persons to carry out investigation, and organized in person experts to discuss the protection program; cultural committee of the city also directly participated in the discussion and provided vigorous support to series works afterwards such as the exhibition.

2008年8月，蔡元培故居修缮保护工程顺利竣工并通过正式验收。修缮后的故居排除了文物险情、恢复了历史原貌，增加了展陈面积，开辟了参观通道，真正实现了名人故居的社会价值，成为金宝街上一处重要的人文景观，更是北京市东城区一处保护名人故居的典范。与此同时，经过十年的精心建设，在金宝街这条西连王府井，东接雅宝路，与CBD相望，全长730米的大街上，已形成由丽晶、丽亭、励竣、鑫海锦江四座豪华酒店，金宝大厦、华丽大厦、东城

1 故居前院
The front yard of the former residence

2 故居中院
The central yard of the former residence

2 故居长廊
The long corridor of the former residence

区行政服务中心等四座甲级写字楼，香港马会北京会所、金宝汇购物中心、酒店式涉外公寓等顶级商业物业组成的高端商圈。灰墙黛瓦、红门绿窗的蔡元培故居，在众多现代化高楼大厦簇拥下，如同镶嵌在星光闪烁宝石中的一块璞玉，沉静、安稳，别有一番风情。应该说，在保护古城与建造国际商业新街区中，金宝街的改造堪称典范之作。而蔡元培故居的保护修缮及利用，也充分体现了富华国际集团对中国文化遗产高度负责的精神和态度，体现了富华国际集团的集体智慧，为企业参与社会公益文化事业探索了新模式，成为企业关心支持文物资源保护利用的成功典范。

In August 2008, the renovation and protection of Cai Yuanpei's former residence was completed smoothly and passed the formal acceptance.

故居后院
The back yard of the former residence

贺　信

北京市东城区人民政府、富华国际集团：

值北京蔡元培故居及蔡元培先生史料陈列馆开馆之际，谨致以衷心的祝贺，并向东城区政府及慷慨出资支持此项工作的富华国际集团表示由衷的感谢和钦佩之意。

蔡元培先生是我国近代著名的民主革命家和教育家，曾在担任北京大学校长期间居住于此，特别是五四运动爆发时，在此居住和生活，因此可以说这里是五四运动的见证者，也是蔡元培先生改革北京大学的历程的证明人，他的"兼容并包，兼收并蓄"教育思想为中国民主革命播下了种子，为近代中国社会发展与进步做出了卓越的成就。

长期以来，北京蔡元培故居处于年久失修状态，此次东城区人民政府和富华国际集团从保护文物、宏扬文化的角度出发，大力进行故居原貌恢复工作并建立陈列馆，这对发扬蔡元培先生精神和开展爱国主义教育都起到了积极地推动作用，你们的工作一定会受到社会的褒扬。

全国政协委员
致公党中央常委
同济大学国际文化交流学院院长

蔡建国

二〇〇九年五月一日

1 集团领导与蔡元培先生亲属研究陈列方案（左一富华金宝房地产有限公司总经理王守元、左二、蔡元培先生的侄曾孙蔡建国、富华国际集团总裁赵勇）
The leaders of Fu Wah International Group discussing the exhibition plan with Mr. Cai's relatives (from the left: Wang Shouyuan, the General Manager of Fu Wah Jinbao Real Estate Co., Ltd., Cai Jianguo, the great grandnephew of Mr. Cai Yuanpei, Chiu Yung, the President of Fu Wah International Group)

2 蔡元培先生的侄曾孙蔡建国先生写信祝贺蔡元培故居对公众开放
Cai Jianguo, the great grandnephew of Mr. Cai Yuanpei was writing a letter to congratulate Cai's former residence opening to the public.

富华国际集团主席陈丽华视察修缮后的蔡元培故居
Chan Laiwa, Chairman of Fu Wah International Group, was inspecting the repaired former residence of Cai Yuanpei.

The renovated old residence eliminated potential dangers in cultural relics, restored its original outlook, increased the display and exhibition area, opened visiting passage, and realized in a true sense the social value of the old residence of celebrities. Hence, it became an important cultural landscape on Jinbao Street, and even a model of protection of celebrities' old residences of Dongcheng District. Meanwhile, after ten years' elaborate construction, a high-end business circle had been developed on the 730-meter-long Jinbao Street that adjoins Wang Fujing in the west, Yabao road in the east, and faces CBD across the road. The circle includes 4 deluxe hotels, namely Regent Beijing, Park Plaza Wangfujing Beijing, Legendale Hotel and Xinhai Jinjiang Hotel, four Grade-A office buildings, like Jinbao Tower, Huali Building, Dongcheng Administrative Service Center, and top commercial properties such as Hong Kong Jockey Club, Jinbao Place shopping center and hotel-type foreign apartments. Among numerous modern high buildings, Cai Yuanpei's old residence, with its grey wall and tilts, red door and green windows,

2009年5月10日，修缮一新的蔡元培故居正式对公众开放
The official opening of the former residence of Cai Yuanpei to the public on May 10, 2009

is like a pure jade set in dazzling gem, calm, steady, unique in style. The renovation of Jinbao Street can be called a model in terms of protecting ancient towns and building international business streets. The protection, repair and use of Cai Yuanpei's former residence fully reflects the highly responsible spirit and attitude of Fu Wah International Group for Chinese cultural heritage, embodies the group's collective wisdom, explores a new pattern for enterprises to participate in social welfare and cultural cause, and becomes a successful example of enterprises that are concerned about and support the protection and use of cultural relics resources.

为蔡元培像揭幕 左起（ 左一：时任东城区政协主席吴弘勇、左二：富华国
际集团主席陈丽华、左三：东城区区委书记杨柳荫、右一：时任东城区人大
常委会主任刘鹏庆、右三：中国载人航天工程办公室副主任杨利伟、右四：
北京市文物局局长孔繁峙）

The unveiling of statue of Cai Yuanpei
(from the left: Wu Hongyong, the then Chairman of the CPPCC
Dongcheng District, Chan Laiwa, Chairman of the Fu Wah International
Group, Yang Liuyin, Secretary of Commission of Dongcheng District;
from the right: Liu Pengqing, the then Chairman of Standing Committee
of the Dongcheng District People's Congress, Yang Liwei, Vice Director
of China Manned Space Engineering Office, Kong Fanzhi, Director of
Beijing Municipal Administration of Cultural Heritage)

为使故居更好地发挥社会价值，富华国际集团聘请北京文博学院的陈步一院长负责故居的展陈设计，并委派专人搜集史料和老物件，恢复再现了蔡元培先生的书房和卧室。修缮后的故居在原有格局的基础上新增了蔡元培先生生平展示厅，展厅内设展板11块，展出相关历史照片50余帧，并通过各种渠道收集与蔡元培先生有关的各个时期的重要历史文献及手稿等，包括蔡元培1936年为呼吁国人抗日写下的墨宝"中国为一人，天下为一家"，以及蔡元培先生手书的五言诗句"平生喜登高，醉眼无疆界"等，将一个充满故事和历史感的蔡元培故居纪念馆回馈给社会。其中很多珍贵资料都是由北京大学档案馆、新文化运动纪念馆和北京市第27中学提供，27中的前身为蔡元培创办的孔德学校，在故居开幕那一天，由27中学的学生志愿者作为蔡元培生平展的讲解员，颇有意义。

In order to better exert the social value of the old residence, Fu Wah International Group engaged Chen Buyi, dean of College of Cultural Relics and Archaeology, to take charge of the design of the exhibition of the residence, and assigned special persons to collect historic materials and old articles to represent the study

故居展厅一隅
A corner of the exhibition hall

and bedroom of Mr. Cai Yuanpei. In the renovated old residence, an exhibition hall of the life of Mr. Cai Yuanpei is added on the basis of the original pattern. There are 11 exhibition boards in the hall, more than 50 historic photos are on show. Moreover, important historic literature and manuscripts of various periods of Mr. Cai Yuanpei were collected through various channels, such as the handwriting of Cai Yuanpei "China is one person, the whole country is a family" in 1936 calling on people to defend against the Japanese and the poem with five characters "Love for climbing height in my life, no boundary in my drunk eyes", bringing an old residence full

of stories and historic senses to the society. Among them, many valuable materials were provided by New Culture Movement Memorial Museum and Beijing 27 Secondary School that grew out of Kong De school founded by Cai Yuanpei. At the opening ceremony of the old residence, students volunteers of Beijing 27 Secondary School acted as the interpreter of life of Cai Yuanpei, which was quite significant.

蔡元培故居书房摆设的英文打字机、电话等老物件都是专门去香港古董市场购置的同时代旧物，希望通过这些物品，引导观众体会那个时代。为了方便观众参观，沿院墙还扩建了一条长32米的走廊。用陈丽华的话说："我们保护蔡元培故居，是抱着最虔诚的心，没有半点的投机。"

The antiques in the study of Cai Yuanpei, such as English typewriter and telephone, were specially purchased from the antique market of Hong Kong. It is wished that these antiques would guide visitors to walk into that

故居书房陈设
The layout of study of the former residence

age. To provide convenience for visitors, a corridor of 32 meters length was also expanded along the walls of the yard. Just as Chan Laiwa said, "We protect the old residence of Cai Yuanpei with the utmost piety and without the slightest motivation of speculation.

故居书房陈设
The layout of study of the former residence

东堂子胡同75号院 No. 75 Yard in Dongtangzizhutong Alleway

故居卧室陈设
The layout of bedroom of the former residence

1　　　　　　　　　　　　　　　　2

2009年5月10日，时隔蔡元培先生离京86年之后，东堂子胡同75号院第一次真正以蔡元培故居的名义向世人敞开了大门。依原貌恢复的卧室里陈设简单，摆放的单人床上铺着蓝底白花的床单、衣架上挂着一件青色的长袍，好像主人刚刚外出的样子。阳光透过书房的窗户，直射在窗前书桌上那台老式的英文打字机上，那是从香港淘来的20世纪初的古董。书桌上文房四宝，还留有当年蔡元培先生编写的《教育心理学大意》的手稿，依稀还散发着淡淡的墨香。书房的一角，一个老旧的转轮拨号电话机也是1918年产的老古董，拿起听筒，里面竟然能听到清晰的拨号的声音。一切都恍如隔世，仿佛它的主人从未走远……

On May 10, 2009, 86 years after Mr. Cai Yuanpei left Beijing, No. 75 yard in Dongtangzihutong alley opened its door to the public in the name of the former residence of Cai Yuanpei for the first time. In the bedroom restored based on its original outlook, the furnishings are very simple. There is a blue-base bed sheet dotted with white flowers on the single bed, a blue robe is hanging at the clothes rack, as if the owner

1、2 接待各国学生参观团
The reception of student's tour groups all over the world

3、27中学的学生利用假期时间来故居做义务讲解员
The students from No.27 Middle School were voluntarily sparing their holiday to be commentators in the former residence.

has just left. The sunshine penetrating through the window of the study shines directly onto the old English typewriter, an antique of last century hunted from Hong Kong, on the desk in front of the window. There are the four treasures of the study, i.e. brush pen, ink-stick, paper and inkstone, and the manuscript of Outlines of Education Psychology compiled by Mr. Cai Yuanpei, which still sends out the light scent of ink vaguely. At a corner of the study, an old and worn rotary telephone was also an antique produced in 1918. Holding the headphone, one can hear clear sound of dialing. All seem like in the remote past, the host never walked far away…

2011年3月7日，东堂子胡同75号院蔡元培故居被列为北京市第八批市级文物保护单位，因其与五四新文化运动的历史渊源，成为吸引公众免费参观的爱国主义教育基地。这座普普通通的小院，如喧嚣中一处清幽的净土，它凝聚着那段风云岁月，它点燃了五四运动最初的星火，它见证了一个民族在面临死亡之际曾经爆发的血性和激昂的良知。百年沧桑，它依然静静地伫立在这里，接受着人们对它往昔的凭吊和缅怀。故居的深处，矗立着一座蔡元培先生的半身汉白玉雕像，正以他深邃的目光，卓越的思想，注视着、期待着并启迪着这个辛亥革命百年后现代的中国。

On March 7, 2011, the former residence of Cai Yuanpei at No. 75 yard in Dongtangzi alley was listed into the eighth batch of city-level units of cultural relics protection of Beijing. It has become a patriotic education base that attracts the public to visit for free because of its historic origin of May 4th Movement and New Culture Movement. This ordinary courtyard, like a pure land amongst the uproar, condenses that turbulent age, ignited the initial fire of May 4th

青少年教育基地，让五四精神永存
The base for teenagers' education. The spirit of May 4 lasts forever

Movement, and witnessed the courage and uprightness and passionate conscience of a nation ever burst out in face of death. Through a century's changes, it still stands there quietly for people to recall and memorize. Deep in the residence stands the white marble upper—body statue of Mr. Cai Yuanpei. He is watching, expecting and inspiring the modern China 100 years after the 1911 revolution with a distant look and prominent thinking.

参考文献

References

《自写年谱》手稿，1940年。

沈尹默：《我和北大》，《文史资料选辑》第61辑，中华书局1979年版。

王云五：《蔡孑民先生与我》，《蔡元培纪念集》第422页，浙江教育出版社1998年版。

1919年5月16日《时报》。

《我在教育界的经验》，《宇宙风》1937年第55期。

孙常炜：《蔡元培先生年谱传记》中册第502——503页，台北国史馆1986年版。

《新教育》1922年第4卷第3期。

《北京大学月刊发刊词》。

蔡元培：《北京大学之进德会旨趣书》，《蔡孑民先生言行录》第172页。

何思源：《五四运动回忆》，《北京文史资料选编》第4辑第67页。

梁敬錞：《五四运动之回忆》，台湾《传记文学》第40卷第5期。

1922年6月12日《晨报》。

萧瑜：《毛泽东和我》第56页，台湾源成文化图书供应社1976年版。

《东方杂志》1934年第31卷第1号。

沈迈士：《怀念蔡元培先生》，《蔡元培纪念集》第216页，浙江教育出版社1998年版。

北京大学档案馆　梁柱　赵存生：《博大坚贞　化腐为奇》。

后记
Postscript

王守元 ┃ 富华永利实业有限公司总经理
Wang Shouyuan
General Manager of Fu Wah Yongli Industrial Co., Ltd.

◆ 蔡元培故居位于北京市东城区东堂子胡同75号院。1986年6月东城区人民政府将其公布为"蔡元培故居",并正式挂牌,属区级文物保护单位。当时该院房产属东城区房管局的直管公房,总计房屋28间,399.7平方米,为三进四合院,并有14户居民在此居住、房屋状况属年久失修的破旧危房。院内私搭乱建情况严重,环境极差,破坏了原有四合院的风貌。

◆ 蔡元培先生,曾出任南京临时政府教育总长,于公元1917年初从法国回到北京担任北京大学校长一职,一直到1923年辞去北大校长的职务离京。东堂子胡同75号院,便是蔡元培先生在此期间的住所。除此,他在北京住过的地方还有多处,像西城区的背阴胡同,宣武区的绳匠胡同,而后来将他在东堂子胡同的这处住处定为其故居,有着十分特殊的意义,那就是因为它与那场震惊中外的五四运动有着直接的关联。

修缮前的故居全貌
The panorama of Cai Yuanpei's former resident before repair

修缮后的故居全貌
The panorama of Cai Yuanpei's
former resident after repair

◆　但是由于历史的原因，蔡元培故居几十年来一直被当成普通民居使用，全然看不到一丝故居当年的格局和影子，接待社会各界参观更是无从提起。

◆　1998年香港富华国际集团在香港与东城区政府签约，负责投资开发建设金宝街，当时明确该项目属"市政带危改"项目，即先打通一条从金鱼胡同东口至雅宝路修建一条40米宽的市政道路，而后引进大市政七条管线，在此基础上对新开通的金宝街南北两侧进行开发建设（即危旧房改造）。在其总体规划中明确，南北两侧共8个开发地块：即北侧为1、2、3、4地块，南侧为5、6、7、8地块，并明确蔡元培故居为文物保护单位。而蔡元培故居就在金宝街南侧的5号地范围内，对当时这一区级挂牌文物保护单位，实则所谓有名无实。如何当时金宝街起步阶段真是难上加难，为什么难主要有下列事项需一一解决才能实现真正的保护。

◆　问题之一：保护的规划方案。涉及：①原地保护；②异地保护；③如需原地保护，是与新建楼宇形成一体，还是新楼与旧舍各自独立。这些需要认真研究，还要请专家进行论证，形成统一的意见后才能上报规划方案。

◆ 问题之二：原蔡元培故居是一处居住14户居民，破烂不堪，私搭乱建严重的大杂院，必须投巨资，将14户居民迁出，才能进行修缮保护工作，此事谈何容易。

◆ 问题之三：保护工程进行之前，需进行房屋普查，制定出修旧如旧的修缮保护方案，报市、区文委批准之后才能施工。

◆ 问题之四：保护修缮方案批准后，依据批复，需进行开工前的各项准备工作。这种开工前的准备工作非同一般，包括组建专业施工队伍，深化施工图纸，准备各项建筑材料等方面的事项都有特殊要求，必须做到一切落实之后，才能确保施工顺利进行。

◆ 问题之五：竣工验收这是要求很高的一项必经的过程，只有顺利通过相关部门验收工作，复杂的修缮保护工程才能画上句号。

◆ 问题之六：筹备布展，搜寻资料，为故居对外开放做好准备。筹备布展，搜寻资料对我们来说真是一个空白点，工作难度非同一般，要达到布展的标准，具备对外开放的条件，是十分困难的工作，不过再难也得解决，尊重历史之情，才能还原历史之实。否则，对外开放就成为一句空谈。

◆ 总之，对蔡元培故居实现完整的保护工作，上述六个方面的问题是不可回避的，每一个问题，每一个阶段得不到妥善解决，其整体推进就无法实现。上述工作可谓是攻坚战，我们从头到尾整整干了五年。

◆ 面对上述实际，富华集团从上到下高度关注，不惜人力、物力、财力的大量投入，在市、区两级政府的领导下，市、区文物主管部门及古建专家的积极参与下，经过从最初的现状调查、专家论证、原址保留、新旧独立、规划审批、到居民拆迁、房屋普查鉴定、制定修缮方案、庭院绿化、古树保护以及报批手续等一系列的努力后，蔡元培故居修复工程终于在2007年7月正式动工。

◆ 在施工中我们本着"保护文物，修旧如旧"的原则，克服了很多困难。名人故居的修复不同于一般的古建修复，如何做到建筑本身的再造符合当时年代的要求，这就需要建设者了解那段特定历史时期的人文、民俗等多方面的知识。在开工之前，集团主席陈丽华女士就明确表示，拆下来的一砖一瓦都不能损毁，要分门别类的登记标号妥善保

利用传统工艺进行修缮
Traditional craftsmanship used in restoration

利用传统工艺进行修缮
Traditional craftsmanship used in restoration

存。指示我们请来古建方面的专家给施工队伍进行业务培训和技术指导，像在施工过程中遇到的木作中的柱子"墩接"、"打钎拨正"、瓦作中的"博缝山"、"代刀灰"、"五进五出"、"五檩十八档"等工艺，一切都得按照旧时的规矩施工，这样才能达到修旧如旧的效果。

◆ 除了技术上的严格把关，资金上投入也是非常大的一笔，仅就院里14户居民的搬迁就不是个小数目。在这一点上，集团主席陈丽华和总裁赵勇是不惜投入，再三强调不给政府增加任何负担，所有修缮费用及其他投入均由富华国际集团解决。从规划布局到修缮保护，集团领导都给予了极大地热情，经常亲临现场，指挥监督。赵勇总裁本身毕业于北大，蔡元培校长又被北大学子称之为"永远的校长"，所以他对这个项目倾注了很多的精力和感情。

◆ 经过两年多的努力，故居的修复工程如期出色地完成。整个故居基本上作到了修旧如旧，返璞归真，恢复传统，还原了历史原貌。正如在工程总结会上所作的总结：蔡元培故居的修缮工作，能取得这样的成果，是"全员努力，领导支持，行业把关，专业指导，精心操作，一丝不苟"的结果。时任主管市长的汪光焘同志更是给予了高度的评价，他曾先后两次到现场视察，多次听取专家论证，并称富华国际集团对金宝街的改造工程兼具传统和现代，尤其是对蔡元培故居的保护有着极其重要的示范作用。

◆ 竣工交用通过正式验收之后，接着又马不停蹄地转入搜寻资料、筹备布展的工作当中。围绕蔡元培故居的实际布局，将故居分为以下几个部分：第一部分是修缮一新的传统四合院布局；第二部分是东边新增走廊窗口的文物展示；第三部分是三进院北房蔡元培先生生平展；第四部分是依照原貌复原的蔡元培先生的办公室和卧室以及蔡元培先生的半身汉白玉雕像。在这里我要特别介绍一下这座汉白玉的雕像，为了再现真实，当时我们费了很多心血，先后去北京大学、李大钊纪念馆、新文化运动馆去考察学习，最终确定了这座汉白玉的半身雕像，并将毛主席对蔡元培先生的评价"学界泰斗 人世楷模"附之雕像左右。在之后的对外展出时受到了参观者的高度评价，称其"形象逼真，用料考究，制作精良，栩栩如生"。其次在蔡元培先生的办公室和卧室方面，我们翻阅了许多历史资料以及蔡元培先生亲属的回忆，尽可能的复原民国初年的风格。房间内的家具及摆设也都是在各地古旧市场以高价淘宝的方式取得的。像蔡先生办公室用的那台打字机就是从香港旧货市场购入的同时代的物品。特别是办公室里那部老电话至今还能通话使用，历史价值极高，还原了当年的生活风貌。

◆ 在整个筹备布展的过程中，也得到了东城区文委、北京27中学、新文化运动馆、北京大学和北京文博学院的大力支持，我们本着"资料稀有，务求真切，纪念先辈，传承历史"的原则，力争达到还原历史的目的。现在展室展出的图片、文史资料和书刊共有100余件，其中不少是真品。展出后效果良好。此项实践使我们体会到只有投入"真心"才能获取"真金"。

◆ 2009年5月10日上午9时，隆重举行了蔡元培故居对外开放的揭幕仪式。富华国际集团主席陈丽华、总裁赵勇亲临迎接，东城区委书记杨柳荫和区人大、区政府、区政协的有关领导亲自到场。市文物局局长孔繁峙、区文委主任、北京大学、27中学领导及有关专家和社会各界人士出席了揭幕仪式。蔡元培先生的曾侄孙蔡建国先生在施工期间曾来此考察，揭幕之日又发来贺信。

◆ 到今天，故居已对外开放两年有余，总计接待海内外各方人士近三万人，效果良好，反响热烈。这里，我摘选几位参观者的留言与各位分享：

2009年7月11日，中国铁道科学研究院陈之红留言：尊敬的陈丽华女士，此举善莫大焉，功在当代，利在千秋。

2009年8月28日，来自西班牙的蔡元培先生第二任夫人的侄孙女黄孝慈女士及先生孟鲁参观后留言：海内外学界楷模，中国近代名人。

2009年12月2日，上海游客朴道参观后留言：能在北京市的核心部位存此精致展示，乃是首都高人一步的体现。

2010年4月26日，爱新觉罗·恒越参观后留言：立碧宇之圣土，救济斯

东堂子胡同75号院｜蔡元培故居的前世今生
No. 75 Yard in Dongtang-zhutong Alleyway
The Past and Present of Cai Yuanpei's Former Residence

061

民。逢百年之华御，分庭易代。犹有大家万世垂范之功，皇天开宗盖派之德，以资贤良，得彰伟岸。凡吾华夏亿兆子民，当永

铭于心……

2010年7月20日一位13岁的小女孩丁玲玲留言：作为来北京参观的小参观者，我感受很深，简介中的感人内容，难以忘怀，我会记

住今天的参观，我相信以后我定会按他老人家的要求去做，会做得更好。Thanks 蔡元培！ 更感谢此馆！ Thank you very much！

2010年11月15日，北京游客刘培留言：蔡先生故居修缮后开放值得庆贺，但愿京城有更多的名人先贤故所向后人展现。

2010年7月20日一位名叫徐爽的参观者留言：来此参观，感到历史、文化的亲切，后人的追忆对今后的自我教育有很大帮助，

青少年爱国主义教育基地
The Patriotic Education Base for the Youth

做人做事会更好。感谢此馆的建立，使我们有观看的机会，我会记住这位革命家、教育家。

2011年3月10日，中国作协张本瀛，蔡元培先生不愧为一位伟人，参观后更加钦佩他的高尚品行！

2011年4月1日，中央财经大学史纲实践小分队在参观后留言：在蔡元培先生精神的感召下，努力学习做祖国未来的栋梁。

2011年5月16日，来自山东文登的游客季玲在参观后留言：在成事中成人，在成人中成事。

◆　像这样的观后留言还有许多，每个人都充满着对蔡先生伟大人格的敬仰与崇尚。其中有位八十多岁的北大老教授张友仁先生，更是对故居倾注了感情。从2009年5月开馆至今，几乎每个月都会收到老先生寄来的关于蔡元培先生的报刊、图片、书籍等各种

资料。他说他感谢富华国际集团对蔡元培故居的保护和修缮，能有这样的一个空间凭吊先人净化心灵。许多参观者在蔡元培先生的塑像前鞠躬默哀，令人感动不已。

◆　也是基于这样一种让历史传承的想法，在辛亥革命百年纪念即将到来之际，富华集团领导决定出版这本书，《东堂子胡同75号 — 蔡元培故居的前世今生》，该书由"文化领袖 泰然襟怀"、"思想自由 兼容并包"、"五四首魁 赤子之心"、"宽厚仁者 百世伟业"、"京城旧宅 历史记忆"、"富华重建 金宝璞玉"、"故居凝香 精神永晖"七大部分组成，图文并茂。前半部分通过追寻蔡元培及其同时代人的回忆片段，大致连缀出蔡元培先生当年在北京生活的真实场景和人际交往，领悟一个文化领袖在乱世危情中的泰然襟怀。后半部分主要从历史和文化的角度阐述保护故居的重要性和必要性，以及修缮及展陈过程中的真实经历。

◆　特别值得高兴的是在这本书筹备过程中，2011年3月8日，蔡元培故居被定为第八批北京市级文物保护单位，这也是对富华

国际集团投资修复这一公益事业项目的肯定和认可。

◆　总之，通观蔡元培故居对外开放之后，能取得如此好的成绩实属不易，这应首先归功于党和政府的领导，归功于文物专家、学者的支持，还有社会各界的关注。

◆　蔡元培故居原地保留的顺利实施，并由区级提升为市级文物保护单位，是富华国际集团无私奉献的结果，是富华国际集团实力的象征，更是陈丽华主席、赵勇总裁的爱国之举、创新之举，是还原历史原貌的唯物之举，是一次成功的范例。

◆　我一生从事房地产工作，与建筑打了一辈子的交道，管、修、建是本行业的重要内涵，蔡先生故居的保护工程正是"修"字的

体现，作为这项保护工程的参与者和亲历者，我倍感自豪，千言万语一句话，蔡先生故居能对外开放展览、警示世人，富华国际集团"应榜上有名，功不可没"。

◆　以上所述仅是我对蔡元培故居保护修缮整个过程的概括简述，不详之处请予指正。

◆　最后在这里，我谨代表集团领导对为故居的修复展出和为该书的出版制作付出辛勤努力的各位同仁朋友表示最诚挚的感谢！我们今天所做的一切都是在记录历史，延续历史，历史也将会记住我们今天的付出。

Cai Yuanpei's former residence is located at No.75 Courtyard, Dongtangzi Alley, Dongcheng District, Beijing. In June 1986, the government of Dongcheng District announced it as "Cai Yuanpei's Former Residence" which was then officially confirmed as a District Protected Historic Site. At that time, the house was under the management of Housing Management Department of Dongcheng District. With 28 rooms covering an area of 399.7m2, the yard with three entrances where 14 families dwelled is a dangerous house out of repair for ages. The illegal buildings inside the yard and the poor surroundings seriously destroyed its original features.

Mr. Cai Yuanpei once served as Education Minister of Nanjing Provisional Government and went back to Beijing from France in 1917 serving as the President of Peking University until 1923 when he resigned and left Beijing. Mr. Cai lived in the No.75 courtyard in Dongtangzi Alley during his post. Except for the yard, he also lived in many other places such as Beiyin Alley in Xicheng District, Shengjiang Alley in Xuanwu District. However, the special significance to take the residence in Dongtangzi Alley as his residence lies in the reason that it was the birthplace of the May 4th Movement which shocked the world.

Because of the historical reasons, it was used as ordinary dwelling for decades. So the layout and traces in those days can find nowhere to locate, not to mention any reception of public visits.

In 1998, Hong Kong Fu Wah International Group signed a contract in Hong Kong with the government of Dongcheng District to develop and reconstruct Jinbao Street, the project was then clearly defined as the "Municipal Reconstruction of the Dangerous Buildings", that is, to firstly build a 40-meter-wide urban road from the east entrance of Jinyu Alley to Yabao Road before introducing seven pipelines, and then to develop and construct both sides of the new street (namely to renovate the dangerous and old houses). It's clearly demonstrated in the overall plan that there are eight developing sites on both north and south sides: No.1, 2, 3, 4 on north side and No. 5, 6,7, 8 on south side. Although Cai Yuanpei's former residence in No. 5 site on the south side is a Protected Historic Site, the protection of it was actually meaningless. The issue of protection was really hard at the beginning of the project only if the following things should be mainly solved one by one.

First: the plan of protection which involves the conservation of the original site; off-site protection; and If needed, whether the former residence integrates with the new buildings or stands independent. These all need careful consideration and also professional proof before making a unified decision and submitting the plan.

Second: the former residence was a broken and old compound resided by 14 households. A huge investment was required to move out the 14 families before the start of the repair and protection project, but it is never an easy job.

Third: Before the protection, the house must go through general examination to draw out the renovation and protection scheme, and then the construction can start under the permission of municipal and district Culture Committee.

Fourth: after the permission, the preparation should be carried out according to the official reply. This phase is very important, including setting up a professional construction team, improving the construction blueprint and preparing building materials, these aspects all need special requirements, and everything must be confirmed so as to ensure smooth construction.

Fifth: the completion and inspection of the project is an exigent and necessary procedure. The complex renovation project comes to an end as long as it passes the inspection of relevant official departments successfully.

Sixth: making preparation for the exhibition, collecting information and preparing the former residence for public visits. We have little knowledge of information search and the exhibition which is therefore a really difficult job for us to achieve the standards of exhibition and opening up, but we have to make it. That is to say, we can only restore history by paying respect to it.

故居中院
The central yard of the former residence

Otherwise, it is impossible to open the residence up to the public. In short, the above six problems are inevitable in the protection work of Cai Yuanpei's former residence. Every problem in every stage must be properly solved, or the whole advancement can not be achieved. The job was so tough that we have worked for five years.

Under such circumstances, Fu Wah International Group paid great attention from top to bottom, making large investments in manpower, material and financial support. Under the leadership of municipal and district government as well as the active participation of the municipal and district cultural relics departments, Beijing university and the ancient-building experts, after the initial investigation, experts discussion, the reservation of the original site, independence of the new and old house, the planning for examination and approval, and then the demolition, housing identification, the making of repairing plan, garden greening, ancient trees protection and series of approval procedures, the restoration project finally started in July 2007.

In construction, in line with the principle of "protecting cultural relics and repairing the old as the-original", we have overcome many difficulties. The repair of celebrities' former residence is different from that of the general historic buildings. How to make sure the restoration

庭院小景
Courtyard View

of the building live up to the requirements at that time, builders will need knowledge of the humanities, customs and so on in that special historical period. Before the construction, the Chairman of group Ms. Chan Laiwa explicitly asked to protect each and every single brick and tile, and to classify and register them with label for proper keeping. We invited the old-building experts to train and guide the construction team, such skills in the construction as the "Dun Jie" and "DaQian BoZheng" "Bo Feng Shan", "Dai Dao Hui" and "Wu Jin Wu Chu" and "Wu Lin Shiba Dang", etc. have to be conducted according to the old carpentry rules so as to realize "Repairing the Old as the Original".

In addition to the strict control on technology, capital investment is also very large in amount. The compensation for the 14 households is not a small number. But Ms. Chan Laiwa and President Chiu Yung were generous in investment, who emphasized to cover all repair expenses and other input by self-raised funds, not putting the burden on government. From the planning scheme to repair and protection, the group leaders have given great enthusiasm, and they often came to the spot to conduct and supervise the project. President Chiu Yung graduated from Peking University whose students called Cai Yuanpei the "eternal President", so Mr. Chiu has contributed a lot into this program.

After two years of hard work, the restoration of the former residence was completed excellently. The former residence have been basically "Repaired the Old as the Original", representing its initial features. As the conclusion in the summing-up meeting: the repair work of Cai's former residence is the result of "joint efforts, leaders' support, serious quality control, professional guidance, careful operation and meticulousness". Mayor Mr. Wang Guangtao gave high comments on the program, who has come to the site twice for inspection and listened to the expert's demonstration, saying the reconstruction project undertaken by Fu Wah International Group combines tradition and modern, and has set up an important example in the protection of the Cai Yuanpei's former residence.

After the completion and acceptance of the program, the staff again turned to search for information and prepare for the exhibition.

Based on the actual layout of the former residence, the house was divided into the following several parts: the first is the layout of the newly repaired traditional quadrangle courtyard; the second is cultural relics display along the new east corridor; the third part comes to the exhibition of Mr. Cai Yuanpei's life experience in the north room of the courtyard; and the fourth part is the white marble bust statue of Mr. Cai and the office and bedroom recovered in accordance with original appearance. Here I would like to make special introduction to the white marble statue. In order to reproduce Mr. Cai well, we studied in Peking University, Li Dazhao Memorial Hall and New Culture Movement Museum before finally confirming the white marble bust, and we added Chairman Mao's comments: "master of the academic circle, model of the world". The following exhibitions were highly appreciated. The statue was praised as "being lifelike, with well-chosen materials and well made". Then, as for Mr. Cai Yuanpei's office and bedroom, based on the historical materials about Mr. Cai and his relatives' memories, we recovered the style in the early republic of China as possible as we could. The furniture and decorations were also gained with high price from the markets selling old and ancient items around China. For example, the typewriter in the office was purchased from a flea market in Hong Kong, which was from Cai's age. What's more, the old phone in the office can still be used, with high historic value. All these help recover the life style in those days.

In the whole preparation process of the exhibition, we also got the strong support of Dongcheng District Cultural Committee, Beijing No.27 Middle School, the New Culture Movement Museum, Peking University and Beijing Institute of Superiority. We adhered to the principle of "though the material is rare, we have to try to produce the truth. To commemorate our ancestors and inherit history", and strive to restore the history. Now the pictures literatures and books displayed at the showroom are more than 100 pieces, most of which are genuine. The exhibition received good response. The practice taught us that only if we did everything with hearts can we obtain a sound harvest.

At 9:00 a.m. on May 10, 2009, the opening ceremony of Cai Yuanpei's Former Residence was held. The Chairman Chan Laiwa and the President Chiu Yung of Fu Wah International Group welcomed the Secretary of Commission of Dongcheng District Yang Liuyin and the relevant leaders from the district National People's Congress, the district government, and district Political Consultative Conference. The chief of district Bureau of Cultural Relics, Kong Fanzhi, the director of the district Commission of Cultural Relics, leaders of Peking University, and the leaders from No. 27 Middle School and experts and the members of community attended the opening ceremony. Mr. Cai Yuanpei's great grandnephew Mr. Cai Jianguo, who also sent a congratulatory letter on the day of opening, had come to inspections during the construction.

The former residence has been opened to the public for more than two years today, which received a total of nearly thirty thousand people from home and abroad with good response and comments. I chose a few visitors' messages to share with you here:

On July 11, 2009, Chen Zhihong from China Railway Scientific Research Institute: To respectful Ms. Chan Laiwa-- Your actions are really significant for the current and future generations.

On August 28, 2009, the grandnephew of the second wife of Mr. Cai,

Huang Xiaoci and her husband Meng Lu from Spanish left a message after the visit: Model of scholars at home and abroad, China's modern celebrity.

On December 2, 2009, a Shanghai tourist named Piao Dao wrote: it means the capital's magnificent progress to save this delicate show in the core of Beijing.

On April 26, 2010, Aixinjueluo Hengyue wrote after his visit: Mr. Cai lived in a great country, and tried his best to save its people. He met the revolutionary change in China and made groundbreaking progress with fine virtues. His contributions to the country and its people were great and all Chinese should remember him forever.

On July 20, 2010, a 13-year-old girl Ding Lingling wrote: as a young visitor to Beijing, I was impressed deeply by the moving contents in introduction. I'll remember this visit and believe that I will act better according to Mr. Cai's requirements. Thank Mr. Cai Yuanpei! Thank this yard! Thank you very much!

On November 15, 2010, Beijing tourist Liu Pei wrote: the opening of the former residence is worth of celebration. I hope more celebrities' former residence will also be open to later generations.

On July 20, 2010, a visitor named Xu Shuang wrote: I felt the kindness and closeness of history and culture. The recall of our ancestors is of great importance to our self-education and also to our ways or attitudes of doing things. I appreciate the reconstruction of the former residence which donates us the visiting opportunity. I will remember the revolutionist and educator.

On March 10, 2011, Zhang Benying from Chinese Writers' Society: Mr. Cai Yuanpei is indeed a great man; I admire his noble character much more after the visit!

On April 1, 2011, the practice teams from Central University of Finance and Economics left a message after visit: Inspired by Mr. Cai Yuanpei's spirit, we will study harder to be the pillar of our motherland in the future.

On May 16, 2011, tourist Ji Ling from Wen Deng, Shandong province: we grow mature in undertakings and make accomplishments when we grow mature.

There are many other similar messages filled with respect to and admiration for Mr. Cai. Among them, an eighty-year-old professor at Peking University, Mr. Zhang Youren embraces strong emotion towards the former residence. Since May 2009 when the yard opened, the old man sent almost every month newspapers, pictures, books, etc. about the former residence. He said he thanked Fu Wah International Group for their protection and maintenance of the former residence which provides a space to ponder on the past and purify the mind. Many visitors bow in silence before the statue of Mr. Cai Yuanpei, which deeply touched us.

Considering about history inheritance, Fu Wah Group leaders decided to publish this book as the centennial of the Revolution of 1911 was approaching, No. 75 Yard in Dongtangzi Alley-the Past and Present of Cai Yuanpei's Former Residence, This book consists of seven parts which are "A Cultural Leader with Poised Mind" , "Free Mind Absorbing Everything", "Leader of the May 4th Movement with Patriotism", "Generous and kind Person Making Great Achievements", "the Old Residence with Historical Memories", "Fu Wah Reconstruction Freshening the Treasure", "the Residence Haunts Fragrance, and Cai's Spirit Lasts Forever". The pictures and its accompanying essay are both excellent. The first half of the book, by tracing the memory clips of Cai Yuanpei and his contemporaries, constructs the real scenes of Mr. Cai's life and his interpersonal communication in Beijing, so as to feel the cultural leader's poised mind in troubled and dangerous times. The second half part mainly expounds the importance and necessity of the former residence protection from the historical and cultural perspectives, as well as the real experience in renovation and exhibition.

It is delightful to know that during the preparation of the book, Cai Yuanpei's former residence was identified as the eighth batch Municipality Protected Historic Site of Beijing on March 8, 2011, which also is the approval and recognition of the Fu Wah International Group's contribution to this public welfare project.

In short, the successful opening of the former residence should first attributes to the leadership of the Communist Party and the government, and to the supports of cultural relics experts and scholars together with the close attention of the society.

Fu Wah International Group should take the most honors who selflessly serve the situ conservation of Cai Yuanpei's former residence which was then advanced from the district to the Municipality Protected Historic Site. This also symbolizes the power of the company and is the patriotic and innovative duty of Chairman Chan Laiwa and the President Chiu Yung, it is a successful example of materialistic action of restore history.

I engaged in the real estate and construction work all my life. Management, repair, and construction are the important content of this industry, the protection project of Mr. Cai's former residence embodied "repair". I'm so proud to be a participant of the protection project. In a word, our Fu Wah International Group is a great contributor to the opening and exhibition of Mr. Cai's former residence which warns people all the time.

The above is only my brief summarization to the whole protection and repair process of the former residence, if any unknown place, please correct me.

Finally, I, on behalf of the group leaders, want to thank with most sincerity the colleagues and friends who have made great efforts for the restoration and exhibition of the former residence and the publication of the book! Today what we do is recording and lasting the history, and the history will also remember our efforts.